DEVELOPMENT CENTRE SEMINARS

WHITHER
AFRICAN
ECONOMIES?

Edited by
Jean-Claude Berthélemy

ORGANISATION FOR ECONOMIC CO-OPERATION AND DEVELOPMENT

ORGANISATION FOR ECONOMIC CO-OPERATION AND DEVELOPMENT

Pursuant to Article 1 of the Convention signed in Paris on 14th December 1960, and which came into force on 30th September 1961, the Organisation for Economic Co-operation and Development (OECD) shall promote policies designed:

- to achieve the highest sustainable economic growth and employment and a rising standard of living in Member countries, while maintaining financial stability, and thus to contribute to the development of the world economy;
- to contribute to sound economic expansion in Member as well as non-member countries in the process of economic development; and
- to contribute to the expansion of world trade on a multilateral, non-discriminatory basis in accordance with international obligations.

The original Member countries of the OECD are Austria, Belgium, Canada, Denmark, France, Germany, Greece, Iceland, Ireland, Italy, Luxembourg, the Netherlands, Norway, Portugal, Spain, Sweden, Switzerland, Turkey, the United Kingdom and the United States. The following countries became Members subsequently through accession at the dates indicated hereafter: Japan (28th April 1964), Finland (28th January 1969), Australia (7th June 1971), New Zealand (29th May 1973) and Mexico (18th May 1994). The Commission of the European Communities takes part in the work of the OECD (Article 13 of the OECD Convention).

The Development Centre of the Organisation for Economic Co-operation and Development was established by decision of the OECD Council on 23rd October 1962 and comprises twenty-two Member countries of the OECD: Austria, Belgium, Canada, Denmark, Finland, France, Germany, Greece, Iceland, Ireland, Italy, Japan, Luxembourg, Mexico, the Netherlands, Norway, Portugal, the United Kingdom, the United States, Spain, Sweden and Switzerland, as well as the Republic of Korea since April 1992 and Argentina and Brazil from March 1994.

The purpose of the Centre is to bring together the knowledge and experience available in Member countries of both economic development and the formulation and execution of general economic policies; to adapt such knowledge and experience to the actual needs of countries or regions in the process of development and to put the results at the disposal of the countries by appropriate means.

The Centre has a special and autonomous position within the OECD which enables it to enjoy scientific independence in the execution of its task. Nevertheless, the Centre can draw upon the experience and knowledge available in the OECD in the development field.

Publié en français sous le titre :
QUEL AVENIR POUR L'ÉCONOMIE AFRICAINE ?

*

* *

Foreword

This volume is produced under the Development Centre's 1993-95 research programme on "The Challenge of National Growth in the 1990s".

The Centre gratefully acknowledges the generous financial contribution by the Government of the Netherlands to this research.

Table of Contents

Preface

The future of Africa is of prime importance to the international community. On a standard-of-living scale, there is nowhere in the world as deep a cleavage between neighbouring regions of the North and the South as between western Europe and sub-Saharan Africa. For OECD Member countries, doing everything they can to help Africa fill the gap — which in the past 30 years has grown wider — is both a human obligation and an absolute necessity.

For economists, it is also an intellectual challenge. While for some 20 years success has followed upon success in East Asia and then in Latin America, we seem to be incapable of coming up with solutions that are appropriate for Africa — despite a mass of research, economic-policy recommendations of all kinds and considerable financial and technological assistance.

The recommendations offered may very well have often been contradictory; the assistance provided may well have been seen, in many cases, as a palliative rather than as a catalyst for development efforts; but we should also acknowledge that we have rarely been capable of designing timely and realistic solutions to Africa's many and sundry difficulties.

The complexity of the intellectual challenge we are facing is largely due to the fact that it is multidimensional. One of the causes of past failures probably stems from not having sufficiently considered the political dimension of the problems. The best recommendations are indeed useless if they are not politically acceptable, as we learned from the implementation of adjustment policies in the 1980s. Similarly, growth will not come if African rulers do not demonstrate a strong political determination to promote economic and social development.

It is comforting to note, however, that in a growing number of African countries, new generations of political leaders now clearly sense their responsibilities and the limits within which their actions can take place. This development should be encouraged in every way, so that the wave of democratic change that broke over Africa in the first half of the 1990s is not followed in subsequent years by a new wave of disappointment.

This is the spirit in which the Development Centre held this seminar, of which this book is the first outcome. To give African decision makers judicious advice, we must call on new ideas, ideas that should include the political dimensions of the problems. I am confident that the conclusions reached during this seminar, thanks to the contribution of eminent experts from Africa, as well as from OECD Member countries, will lead to new and relevant thinking on Africa in the coming years.

Jean Bonvin
President
OECD Development Centre
August 1995

Introduction

Jean-Claude Berthélemy

The evolution of the world towards an increasingly integrated economy in which sub-Saharan Africa does not seem able to participate, the major political changes associated with the end of the cold war and the elimination of apartheid in South Africa, call for a new debate over the future of Africa. The Development Centre therefore convened a seminar of experts on 30 September and 1 October 1994 to consider the contribution that new research on economic policies could make towards solving problems in Africa.

Although the Development Centre does not specifically specialise on sub-Saharan Africa, over the last several years it has published an average of five or six monographs a year on the region. In fact, at the time of the seminar, five projects on Africa were in progress, addressing issues as diverse as the economy of long-term growth or participatory development. The Centre has thus been continually involved in the study of economic policies that would be desirable to implement in Africa. A list of recent and ongoing work on this region is provided in the Appendix.

We nevertheless felt a need for further reflection, in order to give our African studies in the coming years a broad orientation in which the experience of past economic failures would be fully taken into account. This was the central aim, both limited and ambitious, of our seminar: to single out propitious lines of action for research on African economic policies for the coming years, and to try to separate good ideas from the bad.

Before we could meet this challenge, we needed a clear picture of the obstacles facing African economies. The cumulated results of previous research carried out here and there do not necessarily form a whole picture, but the work of the Development Centre provided the outline of a picture, which was filled in for the seminar by Erik Thorbecke and Jeffrey Fine's contributions.

The bulk of the Development Centre's recent thinking on Africa can be grouped under two major topics: adjustment and growth.

Adjustment

In the wide-ranging "Adjustment and Equity" series directed by C. Morrisson, two African countries — Côte d'Ivoire and Ghana — were treated in detailed case studies. These and other studies have shown that adjustment, if well handled and implemented early, makes it possible to improve the economic situation without necessarily changing income distribution to the detriment of the poor. The question, then, is why adjustment seems on average to have been considerably less successful in Africa than, for example, in Latin America.

An answer to this question is, of course, suggested in the preceding paragraph: the right policies have not been applied, or were not applied at the right time. This is more or less the message of recent World Bank publications. As there is no objective reason for African governments to persist more than other governments in applying bad policies in an irrational way, this leads back to the question of the political feasibility of adjustment. Clearly, successful adjustment entails the elimination of a certain number of rent situations. The Development Centre's work on political feasibility demonstrates the link between hostile reactions to adjustment measures and cancellation or reconsideration of such measures — a fatal sequence so often seen in Africa. These considerations explain to some degree the slow progression of adjustment in these countries, where the legitimacy and the solidity of the regimes are usually highly uncertain.

It thus becomes evident that external financial support for adjustment policies can play an important role. Such support makes it possible to "buy" social peace, as was seen in 1994 when the spectacular measure of devaluing the CFA franc was implemented.

This leads us to a second obstacle, one that is still important for many African countries: debt. Excessive debt reduces the chances of successful adjustment, both because it reduces the government's room to manoeuvre in, and because any potential gains for the government from adjustment will come only in the long term. The international financial community has grasped the advantages of lightening the debt of Latin American countries, notably by signing a number of agreements under the Brady Plan. In Africa, however, most situations of excessive debt find no solution, mainly because of the magnitude of the multilateral debts, even considering the grant element of these debts. Analysis of the interaction between the international financial institutions and African governments would no doubt help us understand how debts that can ostensibly be neither rescheduled nor renegotiated have come to be accumulated by countries that in all probability will not be able to reimburse them.

A third obstacle to adjustment in Africa undoubtedly lies in the absence in these economies of an "engine of growth", which makes it even more difficult to share the burden of adjustment among the various actors.

Growth

Research on the determinants of growth, or lack of growth, in Africa by the Development Centre began long ago. A.W. Lewis's work on the economic growth of Nigeria was among the first. Unfortunately, the study, published in 1967, was rendered obsolete by the Biafra war, which points up the vital impact of political stability on growth.

Lewis's study clearly showed the role played by agriculture as the main engine of Nigerian growth. More recently, the Development Centre conducted a series of studies, under the direction of C. Morrisson and subsequently of I. Goldin, demonstrating for several African countries that economic policies have in many cases had a negative impact on agriculture, and hence on growth. Not only has agriculture been taxed, but agricultural progress has been hampered in many ways. In Tanzania, for example, production for the market was discouraged for a long period because of the scarcity of non-agricultural consumer goods, and the adoption of innovations was deliberately slowed down. Of course, the dismal agricultural performances engendered by these policies had negative effects on overall economic growth, as a case study on Ghana has clearly shown.

Why bad policies are adopted is a question that remains, however. To find an answer, we must turn once again to political-economy considerations.

The Development Centre's recent work on growth has adopted a more macroeconomic orientation in order to be able to compare the factors of long-term growth in some African economies (Kenya and Senegal's) with those of some non-African economies. Low levels of saving and investment, which certainly constitutes an obstacle to growth, reflect the low levels of available income, of course, but beyond that, they testify to the absence of good long-term incentives. The customary dominance of rent-seeking activities over productive activities, for instance, or the social obligation to redistribute any additional income within an extended family, are factors that certainly need to be taken into account to explain this.

In the same vein, the education policy of a country like Senegal — where half of the education budget goes to secondary-level and university students while, according to our calculations, only about 20 per cent of the working-age population has completed primary-level schooling — conveys the distortions of a system that for a long time worked implicitly as a training ground for civil servants. In contrast, the case of Kenya, where an endogenous private educational system appeared, shows that in certain circumstances the private sector can circumvent the state for the greater good of the community.

Similarly, the absence of technical progress, which may be measured by the fairly systematic decline of total factor productivity, may sometimes reflect a lack of incentive to progress rather than an inability to master technical change. Moreover, a 1992 Development Centre study based on the cases of Zimbabwe, Tanzania and Angola showed that, contrary to what is generally believed, successful cases of new

11

technologies' being applied and adapted locally can be observed in African countries. Such instances are found only in particular activities based on the use of natural resources, and they encounter a number of obstacles such as the lack of skilled labour. Nevertheless, they provide a new perspective, though not quite as optimistic as we would like, on the long-term growth potential of Africa.

Conclusion

A certain number of questions concerning the political and social organisation of African economies need to be asked, or re-asked, for more effective development policies to be implemented. Two of these in particular are natural complements to previous Development Centre work: Why do rent-seeking activities seem to be more harmful in Africa than elsewhere? What compromises can be reached between political stability and economic efficiency, when the latter must be obtained at the expense of pressure groups? These two questions were central to the discussions of the seminar and will certainly be the object of productive new thinking on the development of African countries.

OECD Development Centre work on Sub-Saharan Africa (1989-94)

I. 1989-94 Publications

1989

Appleyard, R. (ed.) (1989), *The Impact of International Migration on Developing Countries*, Development Centre Seminars.

Azam, J.-P., T. Besley, J. Maton, D. Bevan, P. Collier and P. Horsnell (1989), *The Supply of Manufactured Goods and Agricultural Development: The Case of Ghana, The Case of Rwanda, The Case of Tanzania*, Development Centre Papers.

Berthélemy, J.-C. and C. Morrisson (1989), *Agricultural Development in Africa and the Supply of Manufactured Goods*, Development Centre Studies.

Bourguignon, F. and C. Morrisson (1989), *External Trade and Income Distribution*, Development Centre Studies.

1990

Akuoko-Frimpong, H. (1990), *Rebalancing the Public and Private Sectors in Developing Countries: The Case of Ghana*, Technical Paper No. 14.

Harvey, C. and S.-R. Lewis (1990), *Policy Choice and Development Performance in Botswana*, published for the Development Centre by The Macmillan Press Limited.

Pickett, J. and E. Shaeeldin (1990), *Comparative Advantage in Agriculture in Ghana*, Technical Paper No. 31.

Weekes-Vagliani, W. (1990), *Analyse des variables socio-culturelles et de l'ajustement en Côte d'Ivoire*, Document technique No. 9.

1991

Fontaine, J.M. with the collaboration of Alice Sindzingre (1991), *Macro-Micro Linkages: Structural Adjustment and Fertilizer Policy in Sub-Saharan Africa*, Technical Paper No. 49.

Goldin, I. and L. A. Winters (eds) (1991) *Open Economies: Structural Adjustment and Agriculture*, published for the Development Centre and the Centre for Economic Policy Research by Cambridge University Press.

Pickett, J. (1991), *Economic Development in Ethiopia: Agriculture, the Market and the State*, Development Centre Studies.

1992

Berthélemy, J.-C. (1992), *L'expérience de l'allégement de la dette du Mali*, Document technique No. 56.

Cromwell, E. (1992), *The Impact of Economic Reform on the Performance of the Seed Sector in Eastern and Southern Africa*, Technical Paper No. 68.

Directory of Development Research and Training Institutes in Africa/Inventaire des Instituts de recherche et de formation en matière de développement en Afrique (1992).

Elkan, W., P. Amutenya, J. Andima, R. Sherbourne and E. van der Linden (1992), *Namibian Agriculture: Policies and Prospects*, Technical Paper No. 73.

Jansen, D.J. and A. Rukovo (1992), *Agriculture and the Policy Environment: Zambia and Zimbabwe*, Technical Paper No. 74.

Joumard, I., C. Liedholm and D. Mead (1992), *The Impact of Laws and Regulations on Micro and Small Enterprises in Niger and Swaziland*, Technical Paper No. 77.

Ogbe, N.E. (1992), *Evaluation of Nigeria's Debt-Relief Experience (1985-1990)*, Technical Paper No. 55.

Register of Development Research Projects in Africa/Répertoire des projets de recherche en matière de développement en Afrique (1992).

Roe, A., H. Schneider with G. Pyatt (1992), *Adjustment and Equity in Ghana*, Development Centre Studies.

Schneider, H. with W. Weekes-Vagliani, P. Groppo, S. Lambert, A. Suwa and N. Nguyen Tinh (1992), *Adjustment and Equity in Côte d'Ivoire*, Development Centre Studies.

Tiffin, S. and F. Osotimehin with R. Saunders (1992), *New Technologies and Enterprise Development in Africa*, Development Centre Studies.

Turnham, D., with Leif E. Christophersen and J. Thomas Hexner (1992), *Towards Sustainable Development in Rural Africa*, Development Centre Policy Brief No. 6.

Vourc'h, A. (1992), *L'allégement de la dette au Club de Paris : les évolutions récentes en perspective*, Document technique No. 71.

Vourc'h, A. et M.B. Moussa (1992), *L'expérience de l'allégement de la dette du Niger*, Document technique No. 82.

1993

Alpine, R.W.L. and J. Pickett (1993), *Agriculture, Liberalisation and Economic Growth in Ghana and Côte d'Ivoire: 1960-1990*, Development Centre Studies.

Bevan, D., P. Collier and J.W. Gunning (1993), *Agriculture and the Policy Environment: Tanzania and Kenya*, Development Centre Studies.

Goldin, I. (ed.) (1993), *Economic Reform, Trade and Agricultural Development*, published for the Development Centre by The Macmillan Press Limited.

Morrisson, C., J.-D. Lafay et S. Dessus (1993), *La faisabilité politique de l'ajustement dans les pays africains*, Document technique No. 88.

Schneider, H. (ed.) (1993), *Environmental Education: An Approach to Sustainable Development*, Development Centre Documents (out of stock).

1994

Azam, J.-P. and C. Morrisson (1994), *The Political Feasibility of Adjustment in Côte d'Ivoire and Morocco*, Development Centre Studies.

Birks, S., F. Fluitman, X. Oudin and C. Sinclair (1994*), Skills Acquisition in Micro-Enterprises: Evidence from West Africa*, Development Centre Documents (with the World Bank and ILO).

Brenner, C. and J. Komen (1994), *International Initiatives in Biotechnology for Developing Country Agriculture: Promises and Problems*, Technical Paper No. 100.

Gitu, K. (forthcoming), *Biotechnology and Sustainable Agriculture: The Case of Kenya*, Technical Paper.

Lecomte, B. et P. de Rham (1994), *Promouvoir la maîtrise locale et régionale du développement : une démarche participative à Madagascar*, Document technique No. 96.

Woodend, J. (forthcoming), *Biotechnology and Sustainable Agriculture: The Case of Zimbabwe*, Technical Paper.

Current Activities (1994-95)

Azam, J.P., J.C. Berthélemy and A. Vourc'h, *Growth and Resource Allocation in Kenya and Senegal*.

Reisen, H. and O. Bouin, *Institutional Framework in Post Socialist African Economies: Benin and Tanzania*.

Van der Mensbrugghe, D., *Transition Policies for a New South Africa.*

Schneider, H. *et al., Participatory Development: From Advocacy to Action.*

Conferences

Informal Sector and Institutional Framework in Developing Countries (1990)

Fifth Conference of the Africa Leadership Forum (1990)

Financing Privatisation: Solving Implementation Issues (1991)

Cadre institutionnel et dynamique des micro-entreprises (1994)

Prospects for Debt Relief in Africa (1994)

What Future for Africa? (1994)

Chapter 1

The Impact of Stabilisation and Structural Adjustment Programmes (SSAPs) on Performance in Sub-Saharan Africa

Erik Thorbecke and Solomane Koné

Introduction

Sub-Saharan Africa (sSA) entered the 1980s in a state of severe economic and social crisis, a condition that has been described in detail by a number of authors (World Bank, 1994; Husain, 1993; Singh and Tabatabai, 1993). Annual rates of real GDP growth were in decline and continued to be until the end of the decade and beyond, while in some countries — notably middle-income and those with a fixed-exchange-rate regime — growth was negative in the last years of the decade. Per capita GDP was negative for all groups of countries in the region and gross domestic investment as a share, even of the declining GDP, fell throughout the period.

The agriculture sector, which in sSA plays a key role as a determinant and component of overall economic growth through its linkages with other sectors of the economy, suffered badly between 1981 and 1991. Per capita production growth was negative and absolute growth declined from 3.1 per cent in 1981-86 to 2.8 per cent in 1987-91 (Singh and Tabatabai, 1993). This occurred at a time when world prices for agricultural commodities were also unfavourable, leading to a fall in export incomes from these products and reducing producer price incentives from this source. Domestic policies (trade liberalisation, devaluation, etc.) offset this trend to some extent, but insufficiently to raise per capita agricultural productivity in order to compensate for the effects of demographic changes.

In the industrial sector, a similar picture emerges. While the rate of industrial growth had been relatively high in the 1970s, it slowed significantly in the subsequent decade, dropping to an average annual rate of only 2 per cent (Singh and Tabatabai, 1993). Despite the poor performance of the agricultural sector, manufacturing still failed to increase its share of GDP during the decade in all but a very small number of countries (Mauritius, Zimbabwe and Côte d'Ivoire), and made a negligible contribution to total global manufacturing value added, a fact that is reflected in the insignificance of sSA manufactured products in total world trade. In sum, both industrial and manufacturing growth in sSA slowed down during the 1980s and structural changes to diversify the composition of output and exports did not take place.

As a natural accompaniment to this poor economic performance, social indicators also stagnated or declined. The growth in the number of poor people, measured by all standards, rose in sub-Saharan Africa during the 1980s. In urban areas, even if the relative incidence of poverty declined, it still increased in absolute terms, while in the rural areas both indicators rose. In a context of rising demographic trends and economic decline, real wages and employment growth both fell during the period while unemployment showed a marked increase and the informal sector (where wages are traditionally low) expanded. The only positive part of the story was that the prospects for rural employment appeared to improve slightly, at least in the adjusting countries.

Educational standards are both causes and effects of poor economic performance. A poorly educated work force inhibits economic development, while poor economic performance limits the resources available for education. Sub-Saharan Africa in the 1980s suffered from both sides of this equation. Enrolment levels in all three cycles of schooling, after a post-independence boost, stagnated or declined in most countries. Compared to the dynamic Asian economies, the proportion of enrolments in economically relevant subjects — such as science and engineering — was extremely low. Furthermore, government expenditure on education, while concentrating overall on primary education, actually heavily favoured tertiary-level students on a per capita basis, thus hindering expansion of the base of the system to cope with rising population.

A rather different pattern emerges in health indicators, but even here, in the absence of reliable statistics, conclusions have to be drawn with precaution. Raw indicators, such as life expectancy and infant mortality rates showed a marked improvement over the decade — from 48 years to 52 years for the former and from 119 to 99 in the latter. However, measurements of the quality of life, rather than its quantity, tend to show little improvement, and at the end of the decade access to safe water, for example, was still only available for less than half the population of sub-Saharan Africa. As for the burden of disease, the World Bank's "disability-adjusted life year" (DALY) measure, based upon the number of healthy life years lost as a result of disability or premature death (World Bank, 1993), was 574 per thousand of the population for sSA in 1990, whereas only 178 years per thousand were lost for this reason in China and 344 in India. This would tend to suggest that the "quality of life and health" is significantly worse in the region than it is anywhere else. The conclusion one must draw is that life in sub-Saharan Africa is "nasty and harsh, but longer", to paraphrase Thomas Hobbes. The implication is that a growing proportion of the population is poor and unable to enjoy a fulfilling, active and productive life.

Sub-Saharan Africa's final burden has been that of demographic growth. Indeed, the population has been increasing steadily since at least 1965, and in some countries the rate of growth actually accelerated in the 1980s. Here again, poor economic performance is both a cause and an effect of this phenomenon. Significant increases in development and the standard of living generally contribute to a lowering of fertility rates, while high demographic growth — at least in the initial stages — inhibits development by creating a large, young and economically inactive population, which requires health, education and employment services that the economy is incapable of providing.

Resolving sub-Saharan Africa's social and economic problems has so far appeared to be a conundrum. As a consequence of a combination of a worsening external environment and inappropriate economic policies, the region entered the 1980s facing serious crisis characterised by massive external and internal disequilibria verging on the brink of socio-economic collapse. The response, in terms of stabilisation and structural adjustment programmes (SSAPs) to reduce balance-of-payments and budget deficits and restore the conditions for growth, was uneven and nowhere entirely effective. Why this should be so and what measures could have been taken to reverse negative trends are the subjects of this chapter.

This chapter analyses the impact of SSAPs on performance in sSa from the vantage point of two conflicting diagnoses of, and approaches to, the impact of adjustment policies on performance. The "orthodox" view — best expressed by the World Bank — argues that reforms pay off. Countries that went further in implementing stabilisation and adjustment policies experienced a turnaround in their growth rate and other performance indicators. While blaming poor performance on lack of ,or incomplete, implementation of adjustment programmes, the orthodox approach does concede that reforms were incomplete and that the progress achieved so far is still fragile.

In contrast, the "heterodox" approach — best articulated by UNICEF and its proponents — while supporting the need for SSAPs, argues that the current orthodox reforms focus extensively on short-term stabilisation measures and do not address effectively the deep-rooted structural weaknesses in African economies that are the main reasons for macro instability and economic stagnation. Major structural and institutional changes are needed to complement SSAPs to induce the structural transformations (such as industrialisation, diversification of the export base, and the build up of human capital) without which sustainable long-term growth in sSA is not possible.

The terms "orthodox" and "heterodox" are used in this paper without any value connotation to describe alternative assessments of adjustment. (It is only in Chapter 5 that a confrontation and critical evaluation of these two approaches is undertaken.)

By polarising what may, in reality, be a continuum of different assessments (or at least a bi-polar distribution of such assessments) insights are gained and a more complete and balanced appraisal is made possible. Since the orthodox and heterodox analyses of the impact of SSAPs on performance differ significantly, this chapter highlights these contrasting views in a number of policy areas.

Alternative Methods of Evaluating the Impact of Exogenous Shocks and SSAPs on Performance

Several different approaches have been used to evaluate the impact of SSAPs on performance in sub-Saharan Africa. Unfortunately, methodological problems undermine the reliability of the results obtained with almost all these methods. Yet, some of these methods are clearly superior to others. The salient features of the approaches most commonly used are outlined below. The first difficult methodological issue that arises in evaluating the impact of adjustment on performance indicators is how to distinguish the effects of exogenous variables — over which African governments had no control — from that of policy variables (i.e. the adjustment package). Poor performance could be the result of a combination of unfavourable exogenous shocks and bad policy. In some instances, appropriate policy counteracted what would otherwise have been an even more dismal performance in the light of strongly unfavourable external shocks.

Exogenous Shocks and Performance

The most important exogenous factors affecting sub-Saharan Africa in the last two decades are: the terms-of-trade effects (i.e. the drop in the ratio of export prices to import prices); rising real world interest rates; changes in the flow of external financing (i.e. net external transfers); wars; the worldwide recession starting in the 1980s; and droughts.

At the outset, it is important to recall that the official African view, expressed by the OAU in 1980, at least at the beginning of the 1980s, emphasised the role of these external factors as being mainly responsible for Africa's economic crisis. There is a widely held perception in many African circles that the worsening terms of trade (TT) has been the single most crucial factor in bringing about stagnation in the 1980s. This comes out clearly in the following statement (Mkandawire, 1989, quoted in Elbadawi *et al.*, 1992):

> The results of . . . unfavourable terms of trade have been increased indebtedness which, in its turn, has given birth to crippling debt repayments that are starving all sectors of the economy of the essential imported inputs. Faced with limited resources, African governments have reduced investments in infrastructure, and in most cases even existing infrastructure

is in disrepair for lack of necessary inputs for maintenance. This further contributes to the structural rigidities that blunt supply responsiveness of African agriculture.

What is the evidence? Most sSA economies faced deteriorating terms of trade between 1970 and 1986. Again, this average conceals the differences between countries: oil exporters enjoyed a 100 per cent improvement while non-oil exporters suffered losses of 30 per cent and mineral exporters were hit even harder with losses of about 50 per cent. While these losses are huge, lowering, in effect, the purchasing power of exports accordingly, the income effect of these losses when translated into GDP terms appears significantly more modest. The World Bank (1994) report calculated that for sSA as a whole (excluding Nigeria because of oil and sheer size), the declining terms of trade (TT) meant a drop in external income equivalent to 5.4 per cent of GDP between 1971-73 and 1981-86[1]. If the loss is spread over twelve years, the average annual loss turns out to be 0.4 percentage points. Adding Nigeria to the picture reduces the twelve-year loss to 3.3 per cent of GDP, or 0.3 percentage points a year. The losses were biggest for mineral exporters (about 1.5 percentage points a year) and more moderate for the agricultural exporters (about 0.3 percentage points a year). Oil exporters gained from higher prices, increasing GDP about 0.3 percentage points a year (World Bank, 1994). Other studies appear to confirm the role of declining TT on growth. Easterly *et al.* (1993) estimated that over the 1980s, a negative TT shock averaging one percentage point of GDP a year lowered growth by 0.8 percentage points a year. From this evidence the World Bank concludes that, on an annual basis, "the terms-of-trade decline was small and thus not a major factor in Africa's poor growth record" (World Bank, 1994).

This conclusion needs to be qualified. First, at the aggregate level the reduction in the average growth rate of GDP between 1975-80 and the 1980s was approximately -0.6 per cent, hence the terms-of-trade effect accounts for about two-thirds of the *fall* in the growth rate of GDP between these two periods, but, looked at another way, i.e. relative to actual GDP growth performance (about 1.9 per cent a year in the 1980s) aggregate growth in sSA would have been about one-fifth higher without the fall in terms of trade. The second qualification is that, as always, averages conceal different initial conditions. Countries such as Nigeria, Cameroon and Zambia with large export-to-GDP shares and producing commodities more severely affected by price declines, suffered significantly more than others (Bevan, Collier and Gunning, 1992).

Elbadawi (1992) estimated the impact of negative external shocks (calculated as the sum of the real-interest-rate effect and the TT effect) on sSA GDP in three different periods, 1981-84 compared to 1970-80; 1985-89 compared to 1970-80; and 1985-89 compared to 1981-84; for three groups of sSA countries, i.e. early-intensive-adjustment-lending countries (EIAL)[2], other-adjustment-lending countries (OAL)[3] and non-adjustment-lending countries (NAL)[4], (see Table 1.1). The magnitude of the aggregate shock relative to GDP comparing 1981-84 with 1970-80 was -15.4 per cent for EIAL and -16.4 per cent for NAL which is almost twice the total negative shocks sustained by OAL countries. For all three groups, the collapse of the TT

Table 1.1. **Impact of external shocks on terms of trade and real interest effects as a percentage of GDP**

	1981-84 compared to 1970-80			1985-90 compared to 1970-80			1985-89 compared to 1981-84		
	Terms of trade	Real interest rate	Total shock	Terms of trade	Real interest rate	Total shock	Terms of trade	Real interest rate	Total shock
Early-intensive adjustment lending countries sSA	-13.6	-1.8	-15.4	-13.4	-3.4	16.8	-1.7	-0.6	1.1
Other adjustment lending countries sSA	-6.9	-1.4	-8.3	-9.8	-3.2	-13.0	-2.5	-0.8	-3.3
Non-adjustment lending countries sSA	-15.3	-1.1	-16.4	-8.5	-2.3	-10.8	6.7	-0.7	6.0

Source: Based on Elbadawi (1992).

accounted for between 83 and 93 per cent of the total shock (the remainder being accounted for by rising interest rates). On the basis of their econometric work, Elbadawi *et al.* (1992) conclude:

> 1) the adverse exogenous shocks over the first half of the 1980s have certainly been the trigger that pushed the economies of EIAL and OAL countries of sSA to the brink of crisis and to the subsequent adoption of Bank-assisted type reforms; and 2) the exogenous shocks by themselves, however, do not explain either of the above two developments. The interaction between the shocks and the initial conditions that prevailed in the 1970s is key to understanding why these countries embraced reform.

As Table 1.1 indicates, TT improved in the 1980s. The improvement amounted to 1.7 percentage points of GDP for EIAL countries and 6.7 per cent for NAL countries. In both instances, the positive TT effects were much larger than the negative real-interest-rate effect, resulting in a net positive total external-shock impact on GDP.

On the basis of the above evidence, it would be fair to conclude that the TT effect was a significant but not an overwhelming factor in reducing the growth rate of GDP between the 1970s and the 1980s. Expressed on an annual basis, the depressing effects of declining TT account, at the very most, for a 1 per cent drop in the growth rate of GDP during that period. In contrast, the relative improvements in the TT in the second half of the 1980s compared to the first half had a positive impact on the growth rate of GDP except in the OAL countries.

Net external transfers increased during the 1970s, in part to compensate for the income losses from the weakening TT. Net transfers to sSA (excluding Nigeria) rose from 3.7 per cent of GDP in the early 1970s to between 6 and 7 per cent in the late 1970s and early 1980s. The World Bank (1994, pp. 28-29) remarks that the increase in external transfers compensated partially for the reduction in African GDP caused by the declining TT[5]. Demery (1993) estimated that the net ODA and external transfers adjusted for terms-of-trade effects, received by 24 sSA countries, increased by 16 per cent in real terms on an annual basis between 1981-86 and 1987-91 (from $5.1 billion to $5.9 billion). He argues that:

> In both of the above periods, the increase in net ODA flows has more than compensated for growing debt-service obligations of [these countries] leading to high positive net transfers. However, real net transfers as a portion of real GDP and real imports were virtually unchanged during the two periods (at about 10 per cent and 15 per cent, respectively) . . . The growth rate of real net transfers has been significantly reduced by the terms-of-trade deterioration towards the end of the 1980s . . . Real net transfers [during 1987-91] . . . [declined] by 0.7 per cent per annum on average after the terms-of-trade adjustment.

In conclusion, while it is clearly impossible to estimate fully and accurately the impact of external shocks, it does not appear that they were the exclusive — or even, in the eyes of some analysts — the primary reason for the poor socio-economic performance of sSA, either in the 1970s or 1980s. External shocks played a contributory role to the economic deterioration but cannot, by themselves, explain more than a part of the worsening situation between the 1970s and the 1980s. If this tentative conclusion is correct, much of the blame for poor performance must be ascribed to poor policy regimes, at least until the mid-1980s.

Methodologies to Estimate Impact of SSAPs on Performance

Studies produced on the impact of adjustment in sSA can be grouped into three broad categories: *Before and After (adjustment)* analyses, *Adjusting vs. Non-adjusting* comparisons, and *Counterfactual Modelling* approaches.

Before and After. This method compares given indicators of performance after a specific structural adjustment loan (SAL) was granted or alternatively, after a SSA programme was actually implemented — with the prevailing situation before the programme. The major drawback of this approach is that it assumes that all other things are equal. Given the changes that have occurred during the 1980s in non-programme variables, such as changes in terms of trade or international interest rates, it then becomes transparent that, in the African context, this methodology can be highly unreliable. Furthermore, the counterfactual — the scenario that would have occurred in the absence of the implemented policies — is poorly reflected, since the situation before the programme is normally not a good approximation of it. Thus, a worsening of socio-economic conditions after adjustment as compared to the prevailing situation before adjustment, cannot necessarily be ascribed to, and causally linked to SSAPs. It is quite possible that the conditions might have deteriorated even further in the absence of managed adjustment.

This approach has been extensively employed in the recent literature — particularly by UNICEF and proponents of *Adjustment with a Human Face* (Cornia, Jolly and Stewart, 1987; Cornia, 1991; Stewart, 1992). Most adherents to the heterodox approach to adjustment have used some variant of the naïve "before and after" evaluation method. The intrinsic arbitrariness of this method — allowing a selective use of data and information and being incapable of separating the impact of exogenous factors from that of sSA policies — has elicited strong critical reactions (Berg *et al.*, 1994).

Adjusting vs. Non-adjusting comparisons have been performed in several different fashions. The most crude of these is represented by the so-called *Control Group* approach. Here, countries are divided into adjusters and non-adjusters solely on the basis of whether or not they have received SALs. Hence the degree of implementation is not taken into account. This procedure relies on the behaviour of non-programme countries in order to estimate the counterfactual. Implicitly, it is assumed that the only difference among countries is their participation in the SSAPs; therefore, all countries are assumed to be subject to the same external conditions and their effects. Also, country-specific and preprogramme influences on performance are disregarded. The absence of diversification both within and among groups of countries can, unfortunately, give rise to sample-selection bias.

Precisely in response to these shortcomings a more sophisticated econometric technique has been devised: the *Modified Control Group*. As above, a group of non-adjusting countries is used as a term of reference. In this case, however, the differing impact of external factors and preprogramme characteristics are taken into account. Also, the potential endogeneity of the choice to implement a reform is taken into consideration: the initial conditions that determine the performance in the preprogramme period are likely to influence the decision to participate in a SSAP. Finally, the counterfactual is estimated through a specified policy-maker reaction function.

Although the modified-control-group approach minimises the possible sample-selection bias and controls for important factors not dealt with in the simpler control-group version, it is still not immune to limitations. In the first place, as with any grouping technique, this approach suffers from a degree of subjectivity in the subdivision of countries. Pre-1990 World Bank analyses, which widely applied such a method, have encountered this problem. The first studies on the structural-adjustment impact in sSA simply divided countries into adjusters and non-adjusters, using inconsistent definitions of "adjustment" across the different studies. As Mosley and Weeks (1993, p. 1586) point out:

> The simple rule of any such empirical test, no matter how sophisticated or simple, is that the criterion for the division of a sample into two parts must be prior to and independent of the outcome of the calculations. In other words, there must be a definition of "adjusting" countries which is independent of the measure of success of adjustment (i.e. one must have an *ex ante* division of the sample).

More recent World Bank reports and technical studies (World Bank and UNDP, 1989) tried to improve the quality of the grouping by resorting to a threefold division: "strong", "weak" and "no reform" adjusting countries or alternatively, as in the more sophisticated analyses of Corbo and Rojas (1991) and Elbadawi *et al.* (1992), "early intensive", "other adjusting" and "non-adjusting" countries. Unfortunately, even these grouping criteria do not yet seem completely free of a degree of subjectivity.

Even more importantly, however, the analysis does not measure the degree of policy implementation[6]. Consequently, what has really been tested, as in the two studies above, is the effectiveness of assisted-adjustment lending, rather than the impact of the reforms themselves. Although any measure of policy implementation is somewhat "subjective", without such an indicator it is not possible to assess properly whether policies have worked or whether they have merely been incorrectly enforced (Demery, 1993). In any case, it is interesting to outline the major findings of Elbadawi *et al.*

(1992) and Corbo and Rojas (1991)[7]. Both studies, relying on cross-country regressions, find that reform programmes have had a positive impact on the change in the ratio of exports to GDP and a negative effect on the change in the investment-to-GDP ratio. However, Elbadawi *et al.* (comparing 1985-89 to 1981-84) estimate a positive influence of SSAPs on the rate of change of GDP growth and a negative impact on the change of the saving-to-GDP ratio, while Corbo and Rojas (comparing 1985-88 to 1981-84), with their larger sample, including middle-income countries, obtain a positive relation between SSAPs and the changes in GDP growth rates and the saving-to-GDP ratios, respectively[8]. Incidentally, these studies, controlling as they do for the impact of exogenous shocks (changes in terms of trade and interest rates), found that the effects of the latter on performance were statistically significant but not large.

A different path has been taken by the researchers who have tried to resolve the issue concerning the degree of policy implementation. A first attempt can be found in Mosley *et al.* (1991). Unfortunately the solution offered does not seem adequate. As Demery (1993) points out:

> ... their "compliance with conditionality" variable (ranging from 0 for no SAL to 3 for "high compliance") is only a crude approximation of actual policy implementation. In addition, it is defined only in terms of loan conditionality, rather than the policy changes themselves (some of which may have not been subject to SAL conditionality).

More recently, the World Bank (1994) report on adjustment in Africa has attempted to offer an improved measure. It classifies countries on the basis of an aggregate index that summarises changes in fiscal, monetary, and exchange-rate policy between 1981-86 and 1987-91. Scores from -3 to +3 were assigned to each country according to the size of change in each indicator, where a higher score indicates more policy improvement. A composite score for overall change in macroeconomic policy was then obtained by averaging the individual scores of each one of the indicators. Based on this composite score, countries were then divided into three groups: "Large Policy Improvement", "Small Policy Improvement" and "Deteriorating Policy". A similar indicator was also assigned to account for policy stance. Comparisons were then made using these indicators as a fundamental term of reference. Results of this approach are discussed in subsequent subsections. A drawback — if not flaw — of this approach is that it confuses policy measures and policy outcomes. For example, for monetary policy the index scores were based on the average changes in seigniorage and inflation. The former is a policy instrument, while the latter is a policy outcome (target). It is theoretically possible that a country would follow conservative monetary policies without, in the short run, being able to bring down inflation significantly. In this instance, the country would be unduly classified in the "deteriorating policy" category when, in fact, it implemented the recommended measures!

An attempt to employ this policy-change indicator in an econometric framework is also presented in the World Bank (1994) report. The change in GDP per capita growth between 1981-86 and 1987-91 is used as the dependent variable in a cross-country regression, the objective of which was to assess the impact of policy changes on growth taking into account the effects of external shocks and the rate of growth before adjustment. This analysis shows that policy changes have a positive and statistically significant impact on growth (World Bank, 1994).

Counterfactual Modelling. This last methodology, which deserves mention, is the use of country-specific general-equilibrium models reflecting the underlying socio-economic structure and the behaviour of the major actors (including the government) to simulate the impact of alternative policy scenarios and exogenous shocks. The strength of this approach is that it allows one to estimate the impact of counterfactual scenarios including the consequences of a country's not adjusting, or only marginally adjusting[9]. Different SSA policy packages (and degrees of implementation) can be simulated and their consequences on such policy objectives as economic and sectoral growth, income distribution by socio-economic household groups, and the balance of payments can be estimated. An important advantage of this method is that both direct and indirect effects of adjustment policies on the whole socio-economic system (typically given by a social accounting matrix) can be estimated in a comprehensive, consistent, yet disaggregated way.

The OECD Development Centre pioneered the analysis of the impact of SSAPs on growth and equity based on computable general equilibrium (CGE) models integrating a real and a financial sector. Five country models were built including one for Côte d'Ivoire (Schneider *et al.*, 1992). In general, it was found that SSAPs are not inconsistent with a more equitable income distribution and poverty alleviation (Bourguignon and Morrisson, 1992).

Another programme of research, specifically focused on answering the question, "Does adjustment hurt the poor in sSA?" and employing a country-specific modelling approach, is that of the Cornell Food and Nutrition Policy Program (CFNPP) (Sahn *et al.*, 1994). The state of the economy and the welfare of the poor are compared "with and without" a certain policy change. Five CGE models were built (Cameroon, Gambia, Madagascar, Niger and Tanzania). In addition, two multimarket models (Guinea and Mozambique), one econometric model of Malawi and two multiplier models based on social accounting matrices (SAMs) for Madagascar and Zaire, respectively, were constructed. Simulation experiments based on these models allowed comparisons to be made between the impact of different SSAPs policy packages on macroeconomic stability, growth and poverty alleviation (Sahn *et al.*, 1994). Within limits, generalisations can be obtained by simulating similar policy packages on CGE models of different countries, reflecting different initial settings.

Drawbacks to using the modelling approach to evaluate the impact of adjustment on performance are: 1) CGE models require a large amount of data (that tend to be particularly scarce — if not unreliable — in Africa) and highly skilled resources;

2) these models are relatively crude, inflexible instruments and not very customer-friendly, which means they require experienced and mature analysts to translate the results so that they are operationally useful to policy makers. Nonetheless, it is the best — if not the only — method yielding counterfactual results.

One final remark should be made regarding the role of time in all of the above methodologies. In fact, caution should be used to determine the actual beginning and appropriate duration of the adjustment period over which comparisons are made. World Bank studies often use loan-approval dates; yet policy actions taken before the loan is approved or delays before the policy reform becomes effective can still be present. Also, it is not necessarily true for all countries that the same period of time is sufficient to evaluate the effectiveness of the policies implemented. Results are often very sensitive to the selected beginning and terminal years of a given evaluation.

Major Stabilisation and Adjustment Policies and Instruments

Most sSA countries entered the 1980s exhibiting chronic macroeconomic instability with imbalances characterised by grossly overvalued exchange rates, high budget and current-account deficits, and high inflation rates. Sectoral policies (agricultural, industrial, and financial sectors, etc.) were also characterised by high degrees of distortions in the system of incentives in addition to distortions in the macroeconomic environment, chiefly from overvalued exchange rates. It is widely accepted that broad macroeconomic stability is a necessary condition for both sustained overall and sectoral growth. Furthermore, effective or sound sectoral policies largely require a consistent macroeconomic framework[10].

In order to restore macroeconomic equilibria in the short run and stimulate growth over the medium-to-long run in the early 1980s, most sSA countries negotiated stabilisation programmes with the IMF, usually followed by structural adjustment programmes with the World Bank. Stabilisation refers to short-term policies aimed at restoring macroeconomic stability by primarily reducing the current account and the fiscal deficits, as well as the rate of inflation. Structural adjustment, on the other hand, refers primarily to meso and microeconomic, and to a lesser extent macroeconomic policies aimed at changes in the structure of incentives through changes in relative prices and institutional reforms over the medium-to-long run in order to improve resource allocation, increase economic efficiency, expand growth potential, and increase resilience of the response to future shocks (Thomas *et al.*, 1991).

Although an analytical distinction is usually made between stabilisation and structural adjustment (Cornia, 1991), it must be noted that in practice there is no clear line between the two. For example, they jointly affect aggregate demand and supply over time (Thorbecke, 1988). Furthermore, they are interconnected in the sense that macroeconomic stability can not be sustained over the long run unless major distortions in relative prices and other structural impediments are removed. We refer to both types of policies as either "adjustment", or stabilisation and structural adjustment programmes/policies (SSAPs). SSAPs dominated economic policies in sSA in the 1980s — often to the exclusion of critical complementary measures[11].

Cornia (1991) and Stewart (1992) distinguish three categories of policies in IMF stabilisation programmes: aggregate-demand restraint, "switching" policies and policies aimed at long-term supply enhancement and efficiency. Each category includes at least one major policy instrument. Demand-restraining, or expenditure-reducing policies are measures aimed at reducing or keeping aggregate domestic demand in line with aggregate supply. The policy instruments generally include measures such as public expenditure cuts and, to a lesser extent, increases in revenues through higher fees; replacement of non-tariff barriers by tariffs; tight monetary policies through control over money supply and credit ceilings; wage control or policies aimed at restricting real-income growth; lower subsidies; and a reduction in imports. Switching policies consist in altering the system of incentives to induce a shift of productive resources from the non-tradable to the tradable sector. The main objective here is to increase the supply of exports and import-substitutes and decrease imports. The main policy instruments are devaluation and exchange-rate unification, changes in domestic prices, export subsidies and tariffs. Long-term supply policies are primarily institutional reforms aimed at making the economy more market-oriented (flexible) and at improving its long-term efficiency. These policies are to a large extent the domain of the World Bank. They include trade and price liberalisation, privatisation, and fiscal and financial reforms[12].

Although structural adjustment aims primarily at market-friendly institutional reforms, its macroeconomic component has often included a number of IMF targets with some structural elements added, particularly in the areas of domestic absorption reduction through fiscal and monetary policies and switching policies through exchange-rate policy, for instance.

It should be noted that financing to support policy reforms through structural adjustment loans/lending (SAL) and more recently through sector adjustment loans/ lending (SECAL) has been as crucial as the reforms themselves. SAL aims at providing "fast-disbursing, balance-of-payments financing and support for policy and institutional reforms" (Thomas et al., 1991). While the focus of SAL has been on comprehensive macroeconomic and to a lesser extent sectoral reforms, SECAL has emphasised major microeconomic and institutional reforms in particular sectors such as agriculture, industry, public enterprises, trade, finance, energy and education[13]. A further type of adjustment lending referred to as "hybrid lending" also aims at a sector but with an investment component. The increasing importance of adjustment lending in total World Bank lending over the 1980s has raised a number of concerns and criticisms such as the desirability of a better balance between project and structural adjustment lending, and issues of ownership and transition from adjustment lending (Thomas et al., 1991). The share of adjustment lending in total lending to Africa rose to 48.4 per cent in fiscal year 1992 from 7.8 per cent in 1980. The largest part went to low-income, highly indebted sSA countries, particularly through the Special Program of Assistance (SPA) initiated at the end of 1987 (Husain, 1993)[14].

Table 1.2 presents the main World Bank structural adjustment measures by major policy areas (trade, government and public finance, public enterprises reform, financial sector, social, agriculture and industry) as well as the World Bank assessment of those measures[15]. Exchange-rate and monetary policies, largely part of the IMF domain, are not explicitly mentioned. However, measures in different areas do interact as reforms aimed at a specific area have implications for other areas. For instance, exchange-rate policies influence every sector of the economy while macroeconomic stability is crucial for the success of sectoral reforms. Occasionally, there may also be short- or long-term conflicts between measures such as those between import liberalisation and devaluation.

Table 1.3 shows the frequency of policy instruments in World Bank adjustment loans by major policy area in sSA from 1979-89. It can be seen that the agricultural sector, trade policy, government and public enterprise reforms, and fiscal policy have been the dominant areas of structural reforms. Industrial reforms have not been that important, and have primarily emphasised exchange-rate and trade policies more than specific industrial reforms. Concerns for social policy (poverty) are recent and specific measures have generally been few.

The implementation of SSAPs has been uneven not only across countries and sectors but also within policy areas. One very rough and superficial measure of the degree of implementation consists of estimating the proportion of conditions actually implemented. On that count overall, according to the World Bank, substantial progress would appear to have taken place over time in the sense that about 62 per cent of all conditions were fully implemented with 87 per cent substantial progress recorded in sSA countries compared to 56 per cent and 84 per cent, respectively, for other developing countries. Since many conditions have no "teeth" (e.g. undertaking studies) and do not lead to any immediate policy change, this is a fairly meaningless method of assessing the extent of implementation[16]. In addition to the degree of implementation of reforms, several other factors such as the extent of the initial distortions, external financing, external shocks, and institutional constraints can influence performance.

Short-run Policy Impact on Macroeconomic Stability

One of the first objectives of the orthodox IMF/World Bank economic reforms has been to restore macroeconomic stability and sustain it through needed structural reforms. In the case of sSA, this involves reducing and keeping at low levels the budget and current-account deficits, and inflation rates, as well as depreciating exchange rates and maintaining them at realistic levels.

Table 1.2. **Main structural adjustment measures by major policy areas and assessment**

Policy area	Main measures	World Bank Assessment
Trade policy	**Goals**: – Price reforms, import liberalisation and reduction in anti-export bias - Exchange-rate flexibility and/or devaluation - Export promotion/incentives (export subsidy, institutional development, etc.) - Import liberalisation by reducing barriers (lifting import controls, rationing) - Tariff reforms (reduce the dispersion, the number of rates, and overall level of tariffs), and replacement of QRs by tariffs - Liberalisation input imports for exports - Limit the power of state monopolies	– Real depreciation beneficial in flexible ER countries - More progress in lifting import controls than removing NTBs - Elimination of "rents" generally - Progress in rationing tariffs - Reduction in overall tariffs slow - State monopolies (some political resistance)
Government and public finance	**Goals**: – Reduce (or eliminate) large budget deficits and macro stability (low inflation and interest rates to stimulate private initiatives) - Tax reforms to raise revenues (short and long terms) - Rationalisation of expenditures and public investment through: (i) level and composition of recurrent spending, (ii) the size, allocation and better evaluation of public investment, (iii) institutional change for budgeting, (iv) rationalisation of public enterprises	– Fiscal stance still weak though reductions in primary deficits mainly in low-income and flexible ER countries (importance of grants) - More expenditure cuts; increase in revenues only in few countries (low-income with flexible ER) - Deficit reductions emphasised more than composition of cuts and their growth effects - Tax reform dominated by short-term revenue needs & constrained by weak institutions
Public-sector reform	**Goals**: – Rationalise the operation of public enterprises and their financial drain on government budget - Pricing, investment, and labour policy reforms - Institutional reforms (tariffs, operation, supervision, evaluation, etc.) - Restructuring through training, technical assistance, capital restructuring, organisational and managerial changes - Privatisation of a number of public enterprises	*Overall little progress (needs rethinking) - No significant reduction in number, though growth stopped - Financial performance still poor - Inefficient provision of services - Still poor returns on government investment - Privatisation proceeding slowly
Financial sector	**Goals**: – Reduce or eliminate financial repression (excessive control of interest rates and credit allocation) to discourage capital flight, to mobilise savings for investment, and to allocate resources efficiently - Removing or simplifying the ceilings on interest rates and credit - Relaxing entry restrictions for financial intermediaries	*Overall limited progress; constrained by macroeconomic instability and economic growth - Encouraging signs of financial repression reduction and move toward some privatisation - Slow restructuring & liquidation of bank

Table 1.2 (cont. 1)

Policy area	Main measures	World Bank Assessment
Financial sector (cont.)	- Reducing undue tax burdens on intermediaries (unremunerated reserve requirement)	- Skilled manpower, lack of competition and government intervention constrained improvement of financial infrastructure and regulatory framework
Social policy (poverty)	**Goals:** – Measures to mitigate the short-term social costs of adjustment on poor - Initially, poverty reduction not an explicit central objective of adjustment programmes; Social concerns through Social Dimensions of Adjustment introduced in late 1980s regarding some social expenditures mainly education, health, subsidies	*Overall, more work on how adjustment affect the poor - The majority of poor (rural poor) benefit from more than less adjustment through trade liberalisation and agricultural reforms - Need promoting efficient and better targeting of public spending that benefit the poor
Agriculture	**Goals:** – Improve incentives to farmers and efficiency of institutions dealing with agriculture to induce growth of output, exports, and incomes *Price Policy and Incentive Structure - Increase producer price by keeping it closer to international price and by reducing marketing margins -Remove or reduce input subsidies -Remove exchange-rate taxation (implicit taxation) *Institutional Reforms Liberalise markets for products and inputs or alternatively rationalise the operation of public agencies particularly marketing boards to reduce overhead costs *Investment (long-term measures) - Research and extension - Rural infrastructures (transport, irrigation, rural roads, etc.) - New technologies and better seeds to improve productivity	*Overall, no country has good macro and agricultural policies (ER and/or government intervention) - Increase in real producer prices of export crops in 10 countries, and decrease in 17 - Decline in international prices of most export crops limited the extent of producer price increases - Overall taxation of agriculture reduced in two-thirds of countries. Most countries reduced either explicit or implicit taxation but not both. Taxation increased in both Zambia and Guinea-Bissau - Mixed experience in liberalising export crop pricing and marketing systems (elimination of marketing boards, the best option, is politically difficult) - Some progress in liberalising marketing of major staple food crops - Elimination of fertilizer subsidies slow (removed in about 1/2 of adjusters) though impact on short-run production seems marginal

Table 1.2 (cont. 2)

Policy area	Main measures	World Bank Assessment
Industry	**Goal**: – Efficiency through lower protection, export incentives, little regulation and encouragement of private initiatives - Exchange rate policies (devaluation or alternatively export subsidies) - Trade-policy reforms (import liberalisation, etc.) - Remove tariff exemptions for imported inputs except for export production - Revision of investment code to encourage private sector investment	- The bulk of industrial policy rested on exchange-rate and trade policies - Poor performance linked to poor overall implementation of adjustment - Countries with large improvement in macro policies (e.g. Ghana) experienced increases in production and exports - Impossible to resolve the issue of deindustrialisation (lack of data/indicators)

Sources: World Bank (1994) and various other World Bank publications.

Table 1.3. **Frequency of policy instruments in World Bank adjustment loans by policy in sub-Saharan Africa**
(percentages, 1979-89)

Trade policies	58
Sectoral policies	
Agriculture	62
Industry	30
Energy	12
Financial sector	26
Government finance & administration	57
Public enterprise reforms	58
Social policy	13
Others	42
Absorption reduction*	
fiscal	69
monetary	14
Switching	
exchange rate	18
wage policy	23

*   Relatively insignificant in World Bank loans since they are normally IMF targets.
Source: Adapted from Stewart (1992).

The orthodox view is perhaps best articulated in a recent comprehensive report by the World Bank (1994). The Bank focused on 29 sSA countries that had an adjustment programme in effect between 1987-91 (called "adjusting" countries). According to the Bank, improvements were made in the macroeconomic area (exchange-rate, fiscal and monetary policies) particularly in the second half of the 1980s, and these improvements were largely the result of the reforms though external factors also played a role. However, they argue that reforms were incomplete, and the progress made was still fragile in the sense that no African country has yet achieved a sound macro policy stance, which would mean, for instance, "inflation under 10 per cent, a very low budget deficit, and a competitive exchange rate". Here again a policy outcome is used to define a policy stance.

Improvement in macro policy was judged to have been large in six countries (Ghana, Tanzania, the Gambia, Burkina Faso, Nigeria and Zimbabwe) while small improvement was recorded in nine countries, and macroeconomic policy deteriorated in 11 countries. Improvement in overall macroeconomic policy was generally greater in low-income sSA adjusting countries, particularly in those with flexible exchange rates compared with low-income and fixed-exchange-rate sSA countries. According to the World Bank, the primary reasons behind this difference in performance seem to have been the exchange-rate regime and the amount of external financing, particularly through adjustment lending. Countries with flexible exchange rates were able to devalue in order to improve their competitiveness and they exhibited a relatively better macro policy stance that speeded reforms in other areas, particularly in the productive sectors. Institutional constraints in fixed-exchange-rate countries (CFA countries) prevented this option from occurring until recently. After several years of resistance, CFA countries were allowed to devalue their common currency (the CFA franc) in January 1994, therefore removing the exchange-rate constraint that was considered to be a major obstacle to improving their macro stance, international competitiveness and growth. Preliminary assessments from government and Bank-Fund officials of the post-devaluation period in CFA countries are generally optimistic: inflation seems to have been brought under control and most countries seem to be recovering their traditional export-market shares, previously lost as a result of overvalued exchange rates. Furthermore, there is an increase in external assistance particularly from the Bretton Woods institutions. However, investment is still anaemic and growth has yet to resume. In sum, the orthodox view is that some degree of macro stability has been achieved — though not yet sustainable without a greater degree of implementation of the conventional SSAPs package of reforms. A crucial area for further progress is in deficit reductions since the fiscal situation in most countries is still fragile in the sense that there continues to be heavy reliance on external financing — in particular, grants — to close the fiscal deficit.

The heterodox approach also believes in the need for, and importance of, macroeconomic stability but argues that the current orthodox reforms focus extensively on short-term stabilisation measures and do not address effectively the deep-rooted structural weaknesses in African economies that are the main factors underlying macro instability (Cornia, 1991; Jespersen, 1992; and Stewart, 1992b). They argue that overall stabilisation achieved positive but modest, or only partial results. From an analysis of a sample of 24 adjusting sSA countries (i.e. countries that had an adjustment programme in place in the 1980s) spanning the period from 1980 to 1988, Cornia concluded that only six achieved, simultaneously, the objectives of lower inflation rates *and* lower relative budget and current-account deficits; twelve achieved at least two of the three objectives; while in the remaining six countries, these indicators were as unfavourable as before the stabilisation programme[17]. Stewart (1992b), argues that too much emphasis was put on exchange-rate devaluation, though some depreciation was necessary (given gross exchange-rate overvaluation) in order to provide export incentives. However, devaluation can have limited effects unless it is supported by a mechanism of "structured market" that will allow priority areas (such as agriculture and non-agricultural activities with greater potential supply response) to receive adequate foreign exchange. What is left unspecified is the mechanism (e.g. exchange control?) required to implement this scheme. Furthermore, because of structural rigidities, any attempt to get the exchange rate close to its equilibrium level is not only inflationary but also leads to a misallocation of scarce foreign exchange.

Beside structural factors, the heterodox approach blames external factors, inadequate financing, and a number of limitations and inconsistencies in orthodox stabilisation programmes in explaining the limited success of macro stabilisation in sSA. It also rejects the argument of a weak degree of implementation of reforms in the sense that two IMF-World Bank evaluations claimed that 75 per cent of all programme conditions had been fully implemented (Cornia, 1991).

Medium-to-Long-run Policy Impact on Growth, Exports and Efficiency

Once macro stability had been achieved, the ultimate objective of the overall orthodox reform package was to induce growth and sustain it over the medium to long run. Growth was to come about primarily through sound macro policy and better incentives to the productive sectors (for instance, through expenditure switching, pricing and trade liberalisation policies), mainly in the agricultural sector. The orthodox system of incentives put more emphasis on international competitiveness to encourage exports in the short run in order to compensate for the possible negative effects on output of expenditure-reducing policies and also to achieve external equilibrium. It is also acknowledged that the external balance can deteriorate in the short run because of the critical role of imports in sustaining production in sSA (World Bank, 1994). In fact, this was a major rationale for balance-of-payments support through adjustment lending. Sustainable growth requires the economy to become more efficient and flexible. Efficiency was to be achieved by removing structural distortions in the price system and the functioning of institutions (for instance, through a more competitive environment, reduction in government intervention in markets and productive sectors, labour-market flexibility, rationalisation of government operation, efficiency in public investment, and also greater private initiatives) in the main productive sectors and in other sectors such as the financial and government sectors that support the former.

Impact on Growth

With respect to GDP and per capita GDP growth, the main orthodox argument (World Bank, 1994) is that there is a close and positive relationship between improvement in growth indicators, on the one hand, and both limited government intervention and improvement in macroeconomic policy on the other; and that the contribution to growth of the latter two policy changes/stances is stronger than any other factor, particularly external factors — except possibly in Nigeria, Zambia and Cameroon. Furthermore, a change in macro policy alone is also associated with growth[18]. As empirical support of these propositions, the World Bank (1994) observes that the change in the mean average annual growth rate between 1981-86 and 1987-91 was greatest (2 per cent) for sSA countries with a large improvement in macro policy, modest (1 per cent) for those with a small improvement, and negative (-1.6 per cent) for countries where macro policy deteriorated. In the first group, the best performers, in decreasing order were Nigeria, Ghana and Tanzania; in the second group, Uganda, Niger and Malawi; and the worst performers in the third group were Cameroon, Congo and Côte d'Ivoire (World Bank, 1994).

The World Bank also links positive trends in the other elements affecting growth (i.e. investment and savings) to improvement in macro policy, though the evidence in this case is not as clear cut as in the case of GDP growth, given that these indicators tend to respond slowly to changes in macro policy. It should be noted that although overall macro stability is one of the determinants of private investment, uncertainty and the irreversible nature of investment play particular roles as well. A possible explanation as to why domestic savings remain low — even among the set of good performers — is that large external transfers may be crowding out domestic savings (World Bank, 1994).

The heterodox view relating to the impact of SSAPs on growth is much more sceptical. Based on some evidence of 18 sSA countries that achieved some degree of stabilisation between 1980-81 and 1987-88, Cornia (1991), argued that the achievement of stabilisation objectives has been at the expense of growth in the sense that only five of these countries exhibited positive per capita GDP growth[19]. Furthermore, the fact that structural adjustment has not induced a needed structural transformation (through for example investment in physical and human infrastructure, export diversification, and industrialisation) undermines the prospects for long-term sustained growth in sSA.

Impact on Exports

Again, in the area of exports the World Bank relates growth in exports to improvement in macro policy in sSA adjusting countries (World Bank, 1994). The change in the mean average annual growth rates of exports between 1981-86 and 1987-91 was largest (7.8 per cent) for countries with a large improvement in macro policy (the Gambia, Nigeria and to some extent Ghana were the best performers with changes in growth rates of 11.9 per cent, 10.3 per cent and 3.5 per cent respectively); modest (1.2 per cent) for countries with a small policy improvement (Madagascar, Niger and Mali perform best with 13.7 per cent, 7.3 per cent and 4.2 per cent change in growth rate, respectively), and negative (-1.4 per cent) for countries with a deterioration in macro policy (the worst performers were Cameroon, Congo and Zambia with rates of -25.4 per cent, -3.9 per cent and -0.5 per cent, respectively). Demery (1993) noted a remarkable turnaround in real export growth in SPA countries where the negative annual average real growth rate of export (-2.9 per cent) in 1980-84 turned to a positive one (4.1 per cent) in 1988-90 — at least partially as a result of adjustment. However, there was no significant tendency towards export diversification.

The main heterodox criticism of the impact of SSAPs on exports in sSA is that the former do not promote a diversification away from traditional exports. Sub-Saharan Africa remains overdependent on exports of a few commodities with unstable world prices. As a result, SSAPs have failed to induce a structural transformation to strengthen the resilience of African economies to external shocks (Cornia, 1991; Stewart, 1992). Furthermore, Cornia argues that the impact of SSAPs on exports of traditional products has been mixed on the basis of evidence from 24 sSA adjusting countries from 1982 to 1988. He showed that between 1982 and 1988, real exports increased in 11 countries with annual growth rates higher than 5 per cent in six countries. However, the impact on the balance of payments was not that significant in this set of countries because of depressed commodity prices, and to the extent that these economies exhibited modest improvement in their balance-of-payments current account, it came about primarily through substantial import "strangulation". In the remaining 13 countries, real exports stagnated or declined over the same period.

Impact on Efficiency

The impact of structural adjustment on efficiency relates largely to the extent to which the objectives of institutional reforms were achieved in the various policy areas, i.e. success in rationalising the operation of markets, government, public enterprises, the financial sector as well as the efficiency of public investment.

The orthodox assessment of reforms is provided in Table 1.2. According to the World Bank, some progress was made in reforming institutions with large variations across sectors, but there is still a long way to go to make the complete system reasonably efficient. Progress has been limited in inducing greater efficiency because of constraints such as political resistance due to strong vested interest (Sahn et al., 1994), and weak capabilities to implement and sustain reforms. The most difficult and controversial areas of reform have been the government and the public-enterprise sector, and, to a lesser extent the financial sector. Though some progress seems to have been made in reducing the number (at least the rate of growth) of public enterprises, there remain problems in the public sector overall, such as poor financial standing of enterprises and low (often negative) returns on investment, inefficiency in the provision of services, and slow privatisation (World Bank, 1994). A major overhaul of the financial system may be required (particularly the banking system). The slow pace of institutional reforms tends to undermine the success of overall reforms and sustained growth.

The main heterodox argument of the impact of SSAPs on efficiency can be summarised by the following statement from Cornia (1991):

> Structural-adjustment measures might have increased microeconomic ("X") efficiency and productivity by cutting wasteful investment programmes, eliminating distortions, providing better incentives and through the rationalisation of loss-making public enterprises. However, rapidly declining capital accumulation has represented a major obstacle to the improvement of overall efficiency (which depends also on the "external efficiency" of public transport, communication, power and human infrastructure) and the diversification of production (which requires new investment in non-traditional sectors producing "tradables").

It strains credibility to assume that investment would have been higher in the absence of adjustment — given that foreign direct and public investment are largely financed by capital inflows connected with SSAPs.

Impact of Stabilisation and Adjustment Policy on Economic Sectors

Agriculture

The importance of agriculture in sSA and the fact that it is the sector affected the most by past distortions in macro policy and by the system of incentives (price control and perverse government intervention), means that the bulk of orthodox reforms (in terms of frequency) has been directed at agriculture (see Table 1.3). The top priority in orthodox reforms was to reduce the overall taxation of agriculture (both implicit taxation through exchange-rate overvaluation, and explicit taxation through producer prices and export tax). According to the World Bank (1994), among the 29 adjusting sSA countries real producer prices for export crops were raised in 10 countries while they decreased in 17 countries between 1981-83 and 1989-91[20]. It has been argued that depressed international prices did not permit substantial increases in real producer prices in several sSA countries (Sahn et al., 1994).

38

Given large devaluation in most flexible exchange-rate countries, overall taxation (in terms of the real protection coefficient) fell in 17 countries (the best performers exhibiting a decrease of more than 100 per cent were Ghana, Guinea and Madagascar) while it increased in 11 countries over the same period. The World Bank argues that most countries reduced either the implicit or the explicit taxation but rarely both. It should be noted that the nominal devaluation of 100 per cent of the CFA franc against the French franc (in January 1994) has contributed to reducing exchange-rate taxation and most likely, overall implicit taxation, in the 12 fixed exchange-rate sSA countries, thereby improving their agricultural-policy stance.

Another important set of agricultural-sector reforms has reduced government intervention and liberalised the marketing of export crops, generally by three approaches (World Bank, 1994). The first type of reform, considered to be the best option but politically difficult, involves the elimination of marketing boards. The second type allows the private sector to compete with marketing boards. In the third and most common type of reform, an attempt is made to link producer prices closer to world prices. The efficiency of this system largely depends on the extent to which marketing boards can reduce their operating costs. Côte d'Ivoire applied a variant of this third type where the marketing board has control over the export of coffee and cocoa while the private sector competes in domestic purchasing (World Bank, 1994).

Based on an evaluation of the policy environment in marketing (as of late 1992) and real exchange-rate policy (1990-91) the World Bank provides a classification of 20 sSA countries reflecting their overall agricultural policy environment. Table 1.4, which summarises this information, reveals that the emerging picture is rather dismal. Not a single country scored in the top categories in both marketing-policy and real-exchange-policy stances. The least poor performers are Kenya (considered "adequate" in terms of marketing-policy environment and "mixed" with respect to exchange-rate policy) and Nigeria ("most favourable" marketing stance and "fair" in its exchange-rate policy)[21].

Though reforms in the export-crop sector have dominated agricultural-sector reforms, the World Bank argues that some efforts have also been made in the food sector to boost producer prices and achieve some degree of liberalisation. Furthermore, in order to encourage the use of fertilizer which is very low in sSA, to reduce its cost and to make it more available to most farmers, orthodox reforms have attempted to remove fertilizer subsidies and dismantle inefficient public agencies intervening in the fertilizer sector (fertilizer subsidies often led to rationing and the appearance of black markets with concomitantly high effective prices). The above strategy has faced tremendous resistance, though most orthodox analysts argue that the short-run impact of removing subsidies on production is marginal and that there are long-term payoffs. The main reason is that current subsidies are primarily targeted to already well-off farmers who can afford to pay for them, while small farmers often have to pay the higher black market price. Despite problems of implementation, fertilizer subsidies were removed in about half the adjusting sSA countries (World Bank, 1994).

Table 1.4. **Classification of sub-Saharan African countries
by agricultural policy environment**
(World Bank criteria)

Real exchange policy, 1990-91	Marketing policy, late 1992		
	Most favourable[a]	Mixed[b]	Least favourable[c]
Good	None	None	None
Adequate		Kenya	Ghana
			Madagascar
Fair	Nigeria	Burundi	None
		The Gambia	
		Malawi	
		Niger	
		Uganda	
		Zimbabwe	
Poor or very Poor	Mozambique	Benin	Central African
		Burkina Faso	Republic
		Cameroon	Gabon
		Côte d'Ivoire	Senegal
		Mali	Tanzania
		Rwanda	
		Sierra Leone	
		Zambia	
Unclassified	Guinea	Chad	
	Guinea-Bissau		

[a] Parastatal marketing board eliminated for major export crops.
[b] Some government intervention in major export crops, but producer prices linked to world market prices.
[c] Extensive government control (*de facto* or *de jure*) over collecting and exporting major export crops.
Source: Adapted from the World Bank (1994).

The discussion now turns to the relationship between reforms and agricultural growth. As argued in the World Bank (1994), the overall change in the mean annual agricultural growth rate between 1981-86 and 1987-91 was greatest (1.8 per cent) for sSA adjusting countries with a large reduction in the level of taxation of agriculture, and marginal (0.3 per cent) for countries with a small decrease in the level of taxation, while it was negative (-0.6 per cent) for countries with heavier agricultural taxation. On the other hand, and somewhat surprisingly, there does not appear to be a clear cut pattern between improvement in macroeconomic policy and agricultural growth.

In another study of total factor productivity (TFP) in sSA agriculture — based on a data set of physical output aggregates (where different products are converted into wheat-equivalent units) and corrected for artificial price and exchange-rate effects, Block (1994) found that after 15 years of stagnation, African agricultural TFP increased substantially during the mid-1980's, growing at about 2 per cent per year from 1983 to 1988[22]. In turn, taking the real-exchange-rate depreciation as a proxy for policy reform (i.e. adjustment), his suggestive finding is that policy reform *and* lagged research expenditures explain most of the improvement in agricultural TFP growth. At the same time, Block (1994) argues that cuts in domestic absorption following SSAPs have come largely from public investment — a critical source of funding for agricultural research — and that consequently "the productivity benefits of economic reform may prove to be a one-time effect because of the link between economic reform and technical change . . . Structural adjustment has thus directly undermined governments' ability to invest either in agricultural research or in relaxing the long list of complementary non-price constraints in agricultural growth in Africa".

Given the strong observed association between macro policy (in particular, exchange-rate policy) and aggregate export growth, and because agriculture still remains the largest export sector (about 70 per cent of total export revenues, with no noticeable sign of a shift towards non-agricultural exports), a link between improvement in macro policy and agricultural reforms, on the one hand, and the growth of agricultural exports, on the other, seems likely.

A final point that needs to be stressed is that the generally inelastic short-run aggregate supply response in sSA agriculture suggests that the present package of agricultural reforms (and particularly the emphasis on the right prices) — although necessary — is not sufficient to generate any significant boost in output. This clearly reinforces the case for investment in agriculture and rural infrastructure as a key missing ingredient. In this context the recent acceleration of agricultural production in Nigeria went hand in hand with a higher level of rural infrastructure and investment in research and extension (World Bank, 1994).

The heterodox view as reflected e.g. by Cornia (1991) and Stewart (1992) tends to agree with the orthodox reform emphasis on encouraging higher producer prices, but argues that SSAPs largely ignored, and did not attempt to remove the long-term non-price constraints on agricultural growth (inadequate rural infrastructure, low and declining use of fertilizers as well as irrigation systems) through appropriate measures such as greater public investment in rural physical infrastructure and the provision of agricultural services such as credit or improved seeds. In fact, government expenditure on agriculture fell in a number of countries between 1980 and 1985 (Stewart, 1992b). In other words, the major shortcoming of reforms in agriculture has been the lack of investment, which tended to limit aggregate supply response, which is crucial to the success or failure of orthodox adjustment programmes (Singh and Tabatabai, 1993).

According to Bhaduri (1993), structural adjustment "often reinforced the short-term bias of IMF 'conditionality' in stabilisation programmes instead of modifying them from a longer-term perspective." The heterodox approach also argues that orthodox reforms put too much emphasis on traditional export crops, which not only tended to depress the food-crop sector (negatively affecting food supply, nutrition and calorie intakes) but also harmed the objective of export diversification. This emphasis also has international implications in the sense that it might have contributed to declining world prices of commodities (e.g. for cocoa and coffee) and thus a deterioration in the terms of trade.

It has also been claimed that the combined effects of a devaluation (which tends to increase the cost of imported inputs) and the removal of fertilizer subsidies can contribute to lower fertilizer use, therefore affecting productivity. Cornia, van der Hoeven and Lall (1992) argued that for most sSA countries the "most tragic element [of African government policy initially and SSAPs in the 1980s] has been the inability to manage the transition from a land-abundant, shifting agriculture to more input-intensive settled farming systems."

Industry

The impact of reforms on industry was supposed to work primarily through the exchange-rate policy (or through a "pseudo-devaluation" — i.e. an export subsidy — when a devaluation was not possible, as in Côte d'Ivoire and Senegal prior to 1994) to provide incentives to industrial exports and through trade policy to lower the overall level of protection. In addition, reforming state enterprises and privatisation were high priorities on the industrial adjustment agenda. "Adjustment programmes," argues the World Bank (1994), "radically change relative prices and the incentive environment that firms operate in — and thus the characteristics and behaviour of firms that survive and prosper." Furthermore, the Bank contends that there is a strong relationship between macro policy and the growth of industries in the sense that sSA countries with a large improvement in macro policy in the 1980s also experienced a strong acceleration in industrial and manufacturing growth with average annual median increases during 1981-86 and 1987-91 of 6.1 and 5.8 per cent, respectively (Tanzania, Nigeria and Ghana performed best), compared to 1.7 and 1.1, respectively, for sSA countries with a deterioration in macro policy (the worst industrial performance occurred in Cameroon, Benin, Rwanda and Congo).

Whereas the heterodox school takes it for granted that a process of deindustrialisation has been underway for some time in sSA, the World Bank refutes this thesis with regard to Ghana, Kenya and Tanzania (on the basis of various empirical indicators) and argues that there is simply not enough information available in most other sSA countries to answer this question conclusively. Furthermore, the Bank acknowledges that in order to shift African industry to a higher growth path the upgrading of technological capabilities, skills, infrastructure and business support services (also stressed in Lall, 1990) needs to be undertaken in addition to current reforms. Although the World Bank (1994) does not mention the desirability of manufacturing exports and their contribution to export diversification as explicit goals, it is envisaged that this process will occur more or less automatically through the operation of free markets. In any case, the orthodox position is that interventionist measures should be strongly discouraged.

In contrast, the heterodox school claims that current orthodox reforms do not properly address the problem of industrialisation in sSA which is critical for structural change and long-term development. In fact, they argue that orthodox reforms, through their neglect of human resources, capacity and institutional development (Lall, 1990; Cornia, van der Hoeven and Lall, 1992), and their emphasis on non-selective liberalisation (Stewart, 1992b), have a negative impact on promoting industrialisation. With respect to the specific effects of stabilisation and structural adjustment on industrialisation, Cornia, van der Hoeven and Lall (1992) argue that: *(i)* the demand-contraction effects of SSAPs led to a fall in domestic demand (the driving force in any early phase of industrialisation) for industrial output, and the simultaneous rise in domestic interest rates caused industrial investment to decline; *(ii)* imports dropped in some cases, affecting capacity utilisation negatively; *(iii)* devaluation increased the cost of essential inputs and capital goods; in some cases, external inflows and import liberalisation encouraged the imports of competitive consumer goods; and, finally, *(iv)* the change in ownership from the public to the private sector to induce efficiency did not always materialise.

Evaluating the performance of manufacturing in 15 sSA, Asian, Latin American, Middle Eastern and North African adjusting countries over the period 1979-86, Tybout (1991) derives a number of conclusions regarding sSA. First, he uses a relation linking the growth of GDP to that of industry to show that African industrial producers are the least protected from macroeconomic fluctuations[23]. Second, using a concept of the "normal" amount of industrialisation as the difference between the growth rate of GDP and that of manufacturing, assuming that the industrial sector grows faster than GDP in developing countries, he concludes that there is no solid evidence that SAL countries (countries that received structural adjustment loans) industrialised faster. Third, he finds that World Bank lending and conditionality have mainly served to maintain the economic position of recipients through, for instance, substantial import penetration, and that there is weak evidence that export-promotion policies and devaluation have encouraged export expansion. Finally, he concludes that rapid deindustrialisation took place in Africa given that manufacturing contracted more rapidly than GDP. Based on the evidence that in 1980-87 the annual industrial growth rate was less than 2 per cent in 19 sSA countries, and fell in 10 sSA countries as well as in sSA as a whole (by -1.2 per cent), Stewart (1992a) also arrives at the conclusion that deindustrialisation took place in sSA in the 1980s. The World Bank (1994) does not necessarily reject that argument totally but links deindustrialisation in a number of countries more to their relatively weak degree of implementation of adjustment programmes than to any other factor.

Impact of Stabilisation and Adjustment Policies on Poverty

The burden of the evidence that is available — and it is very limited in sub-Saharan Africa, with only two countries possessing comparative survey information on poverty for more than one time period in the 1980s — suggests that, on an aggregate basis, poverty worsened in the 1980s. The problem with any aggregate measure is that it hides possibly significant differences between countries in poverty and social welfare trends. In any case, the issue is not whether poverty did or did not increase but rather whether this trend can be ascribed, or at least causally linked, to SSAPs policies or whether SSAPs policies had a neutral, or even positive, impact on poverty. Berg *et al.* (1994) put it well:

> The impact of structural adjustment on the poor can in theory be either negative or positive. A priori reasons exist to anticipate policy-induced deterioration for low-income groups in developing countries — for example, through cuts in food subsidies and in employment and real wages. But there are also reasons to anticipate improvement for these groups as a result of economic stabilisation and market-oriented structural reforms — for example, by consumption-smoothing that results from reduced public investment, improved rural-urban terms of trade following exchange-rate adjustments, and greater inflows of official aid following adoption of reforms. If there is a supply response, everybody should benefit from renewed growth.

At the risk of oversimplification, there are two almost opposing evaluations of the impact of SSAPs on poverty. The orthodox approach is, probably, best expressed and reflected by the World Bank (1994) report on adjustment in Africa and by Sahn *et al.* (1994), summarising the results of a multi-year research programme. The former uses a method comparing the performance of countries on the basis of the intensity of policy adjustment and implementation in three areas: fiscal policy, monetary policy and exchange-rate policy[24]. Sahn *et al.* (1994) use an analytical framework that permits an evaluation of alternative policy scenarios on a counterfactual basis, including how the poor would fare with and without policy change, focused on ten countries in sub-Saharan Africa.

The main conclusion reached by the World Bank (1994) report is:

> Adjustment has contributed to faster GDP per capita growth in half the countries examined in this report, and there is every reason to think that it has helped the poor, based on the strong linkage between growth and poverty reduction elsewhere in the world.

While recognising, as pointed out by UNICEF, that many adjustment programmes launched in the early 1980s did not pay sufficient attention to provision of services adequate to the poor, more recently efforts have gone into improving the composition of public expenditure and the delivery of social services. The main characteristics of the poor in sub-Saharan Africa are summarised as follows: i) most of the poor live in rural areas; ii) they rely extensively on agricultural income, which constitutes more than half of all income in most of these countries; iii) the majority of poor farmers' income comes from non-traded food products either consumed by the household or sold locally. However, in many countries (e.g. Côte d'Ivoire and Ghana) earnings from export crops represent a significant part of poor farmers' income; and, iv) off-farm income is also significant, amounting to at least one-fifth of total income in all but two of the areas studied (Dorosh and Sahn, 1993). Given these facts, the World Bank derives the following conclusions. First, although the high share of production for own consumption reduces the dependence of the poor on (and their vulnerability to) market forces, they still rely on selling their products for a substantial part of their income and will benefit from higher effective prices. Secondly, improvements in the prices of tradable crops (following a devaluation) should have a positive impact on the incomes of the rural poor — at least in the short run. Thirdly, any general improvements in the rural-urban terms of trade are likely to result in favourable direct and indirect effects on rural non-agricultural activities through the strong demand and supply linkages between the latter and agricultural activities (World Bank, 1994).

The impact of real exchange-rate depreciation and agricultural reforms, likewise, is unlikely to have had a negative impact on the consumption of the poor. The increasing production of domestic non-tradable food crops in recent years has kept real prices from increasing. The rural poor — particularly the net purchasers — have probably not been hurt. Of course, the net producers of tradable crops benefited from a real depreciation, even when supply response was inelastic. Removal of food subsidies did not adversely affect the rural poor since few of them had access to cheap food imports before adjustment. Instead, it was largely the urban élite (and some urban poor) who had access to rationed foodstuffs at below-market prices. The bulk of the poor had to obtain imported food either from the open or parallel market (World Bank, 1994). The World Bank recognises that in some instances agricultural reforms can inflict hardship on the poor. For instance, poor urban consumers in Madagascar who benefited to some extent from controlled rice prices before the devaluation were hurt by the removal of subsidies.

The main conclusion reached by the Cornell Food and Nutrition Policy Program (CFNPP) research programme on the impact of structural adjustment on poverty in sub-Saharan Africa is that "on balance, adjustment policies, when implemented, benefit most of the poor. Nonetheless, the magnitude of these benefits is too small to contribute in a meaningful way to short-term poverty alleviation" (Sahn et al., 1994). The CFNPP approach is based on the use of CGE and other models permitting different policy scenarios (i.e. reflecting different packages and degrees of implementation of stabilisation and adjustment measures) to be played out and evaluated. Findings from general equilibrium models in five sSA countries indicate that the poor stand to benefit from the elimination of foreign-exchange rationing and the liberalisation of trade regimes. This is because devaluation increases the relative prices of tradables that the farmers are directly engaged in producing, and eliminates the rents associated with foreign-exchange rationing[25]. These rents, instead of being captured by a small group of primarily urban élite become redistributed through the economy — with the poor's being among the important beneficiaries. Secondly, while health and education expenditures have generally not been cut either in real terms or as a share of GDP, survey data on the incidence of public expenditures in these two areas show that governments do not target services to the poor well. Thirdly, budgetary retrenchment, which is part and parcel of the conventional SSAP package, entails a significant reduction in the size of a generally bloated and unproductive civil service. However, survey data from Ghana and Guinea show that the poor — especially women — are unlikely to be on the public payroll. Fourth, there is some evidence from survey data (particularly from Ghana) suggesting that taxation has become more progressive since the beginning of the economic reform programme. In particular, recent evidence shows that adjustment policies have contributed to lower rates of taxation, particularly implicit taxation through overvalued exchange rates. Simulations from CGE and multi-market models show that incomes of the poor tend to increase when taxation of export crops falls.

Finally, it was found that the liberalisation of domestic food markets that occurred in adjusting countries did not, on balance, have adverse effects on the poor because the latter rarely benefited from controlled prices in official markets before adjustment. Some urban poor may have been negatively affected by the removal of subsidies (as in Madagascar) but most of the rural poor in sub-Saharan Africa appear to have gained from liberalisation.

A third very recent analysis (Berg *et al.*, 1994) of the impact of adjustment on poverty after reviewing the evolution of a large number of indicators during the 1980s, covering as many as 40 sub-Saharan countries concludes:

> We *should* be surprised that few differences (between adjusters and non-adjusters) in social indicators are visible, for this indicates that the adoption of market-oriented economic policies in the 1980s did not have dire consequences so loudly anticipated by so many observers. In other words, the appropriate proposition for testing is that the poor were hurt by adjustment policies. What is noteworthy and surprising is the fact that this proposition, which incorporates strongly held received doctrine, is not supported by cross-country comparisons of poverty indicators.

Next we turn to a review of the heterodox approach. At the outset, it is important to keep in mind that this approach evolved largely on the basis of the socio-economic conditions prevailing in the first half of the 1980s and was first systematically articulated by UNICEF in 1987 in its volume on *Adjustment with a Human Face*. In fact, most of the adherents of this approach based their analysis on data preceding 1988. This is a crucial qualification since, in a number of sub-Saharan African countries, the socio-economic situation actually improved in the late 1980s, at least partially as a result of some modifications in the package of SSA policies induced by the UNICEF critique of earlier adjustment policies. In fact, as will be seen subsequently, some of the heterodox writers appear to have become somewhat less critical of the orthodox prescription in recent years. UNICEF recognises that "the primary cause of the downward economic pressure on the human situation in most of the countries affected is the overall economic situation, globally and nationally, not adjustment policy as such" (Cornia, Jolly and Stewart, 1987). It also concedes that without some form of adjustment, the situation would often be far worse. Its position is that conventional adjustment policies (at least those recommended in the first part of the 1980s) did not protect the human needs of the vulnerable and that, consequently, a broader approach to adjustment is required.

This broader approach is to be found by adding a poverty-alleviation dimension to adjustment through the rebirth of the "basic needs" strategy initially developed by ILO in the 1970s. UNICEF in 1987 took it for granted that "incomes of the poor are falling . . . and the burden of adjustment policies often fall (sic) disproportionately on the poor" (Cornia, Jolly and Stewart, 1987). The contention that the poor carry the burden of adjustment was based on very little systematic analysis of the data covering essentially the first half of the 1980s[26]. For one thing, whereas many sub-Saharan countries had received structural-adjustment loans in the early 1980s, the process of implementation of the reform package was still in its infancy. This is one of the dangers of employing a naïve variant of the "before and after" approach in assessing the impact of adjustment. It was claimed that the type of adjustment policies adopted has been an important contributory element to deteriorating conditions — particularly that of children. The process leading to this deterioration is described as resulting from 1) the deflationary character of most programmes that led to growing poverty through depressed employment and real incomes; and 2) the negative effects of certain macroeconomic policies on the welfare of particular socio-economic groups (e.g. through the impact of devaluation on producer prices, rising urban food prices, and cuts in food subsidies) and cuts in social expenditures (Cornia, Jolly and Stewart, 1987). The message was that special programmes targeted to poverty alleviation were called for. Clearly, UNICEF by emphasising poverty alleviation as a major objective of development has brought the social dimensions to the centre stage of the adjustment-policy debate and induced the World Bank to become more proactive in addressing the poverty objective within the context of its lending instruments (Demery, 1993). The heterodox approach has rightly emphasised the relative neglect of human-capital development (Stewart, 1992) and the provision of agriculture infrastructure that would tend to benefit the poor both directly (during the construction stage through the employment of unskilled labour) and indirectly by reducing marketing margins on food.

Finally, Jamal and Weeks (1993) are very critical of what they see as a negative impact of SSAPs on urban poverty. They argue that whatever urban bias might have existed in the past in Africa has by now fully disappeared and that the typical adjustment package strongly discriminates against the urban poor. As evidence, they paint a sharply deteriorating picture of minimum urban wages in many African countries combined with the growth of informal-sector employment and a concomitant drop in formal employment (which, however, has always been relatively small). Furthermore, they argue that adjustment instruments such as devaluation that raise the prices of tradables are unlikely to benefit small farmers because of inelastic supply response and the very inelastic world demand for primary products. Here, again, a qualification is in order: higher prices benefit farmers even without any rise in output.

Conflicts and Complementarity between SSAPs and Other Policies and Reforms Needed for Sustainable Growth with Poverty Alleviation

The UNICEF and heterodox critical evaluation of the impact of SSAPs on long-term growth and poverty alleviation — whether fully justified or not on empirical grounds — sensitised multilateral and bilateral donors to the need to focus significantly more on the social dimensions of adjustment. It also served a useful purpose in broadening the debate regarding the various components required in a successful long-term development strategy within the context of sub-Saharan Africa. While recognising that, in the face of massive internal and external disequilibria, the implementation of SSAPs was unavoidable and clearly a necessary condition to the restoration of some degree of macroeconomic balance, adjustment, by itself, was hardly a sufficient condition, and in some instances, could even be an impediment in the transition to a regime of sustainable and equitable growth. The successful achievement of the latter requires not only modifications in the conventional adjustment package but, even more importantly, the implementation of a whole series of complementary and reinforcing reforms ranging from greater emphasis on, and investment in, human capital and physical infrastructure to major institutional changes — particularly in agriculture and industry — benefiting small producers.

The orthodox approach, at least as articulated by the Bretton Woods institutions, on the other hand, can be characterised — if not caricatured — as being myopically fixated on SSAPs — as almost a cure-all. Intended initially as temporary programmes to restore macroeconomic equilibrium and provide a basis for a new take-off, there is a risk that in their zeal to defend SSAPs against their detractors, the World Bank and IMF may have lost sight of, or have underestimated, the critical importance of complementary measures for sustainable growth to occur. It is almost as if, in certain World Bank circles, adjustment when appropriately implemented, was becoming visualised as both a necessary *and* sufficient condition for opening the door to an equitable growth path.

Cornia (1991) and Stewart (1992) classify stabilisation and structural adjustment policies into three categories: contradictory, incomplete and additional. *Contradictory policies*, i.e. policies which conflict directly with long-term objectives, are identified in four different areas:

1. Conflicts between cuts in government expenditures and the need to sustain or expand public infrastructure and human capabilities. Budget retrenchment normally entails: a) cuts in government recurrent and capital expenditures on health and education that impinge on human-capital investment; and b) cuts in public investment in physical infrastructure — particularly in the rural areas — that is needed for supply responsiveness in agriculture.

2. Demand-restraint policies, combined with credit curtailment and deflationary monetary policies, create an unfavourable climate for domestic and foreign private investment.

3.   Conflicts between undifferentiated and sudden import liberalisation and the need to diversify production towards manufacturing. Sudden and sharp reductions in protection rates are held responsible for the observed deindustrialisation process.

4.   Conflicts between policies encouraging an expansion of traditional primary-commodity exports and the need to diversify the export basket (and stabilise the balance of payments). This type of policy is considered partly responsible for the deterioration of the terms of trade.

The second category of policies discussed by Cornia and Stewart are *incomplete policies*. These policies have both positive and negative effects over the long term. Their positive features are that they help correct past distortions and encourage efficiency. However, since they do not provide essential complementary changes, they need to be amended in order to meet long-term objectives more successfully. A vast array of modifications has been proposed mainly in agricultural policies, credit markets, foreign investment, parastatals, trade, and foreign exchange. An important underlying objective of these amendments is to improve the climate for greater supply response in agriculture (particularly among the small producers), and to improve African entrepreneurial capabilities and experience, while moving the economy towards a structure more responsive to taking advantage of dynamic comparative advantage in non-traditional sectors.

Finally, *additional reforms* have been proposed in areas not presently embraced by SSAPs that are thought to be critical to the achievement of long-run development. These policies are mainly designed to increase equity and participation by the poor in the decision-making process. Examples can be found in suggested land reform schemes in countries where landlessness is acute; institutional reforms to provide better services to smallholders; and, finally, policies to create or improve regional institutions in the field of agricultural research and development, public health, trade, transport and others forms of economic co-operation.

The most critical reform stressed by these authors is the need to accelerate the development of human resources — a key ingredient in East and Southeast Asian growth.

The success of the above set of suggested policy changes is strongly dependent on improvements in the international economic climate. In fact, three fundamental changes have been suggested to reverse the downward path of many African countries: debt write-off by all the major lenders; encouragement of commodity-price agreements through production controls in all producing countries; and an increase in resource flows over the next 10 years to a level at least twice the present one.

If the World Bank (1994) report on adjustment can be taken as representative of the orthodox position, it is disappointing in its lack of specificity regarding desirable complementary reforms to SSAPs as part and parcel of a long-term development strategy. World Bank officials appear generally satisfied with the design of SSAPs and appear to assign much of the responsibility for past performance failures to governments rather than to an arguably incomplete package of policy measures and development strategy. As a result, long-term suggestions follow the same logic that has inspired ongoing reforms. Namely, future adjustment efforts must be directed towards a higher degree of policy implementation, a renewed effort to encourage competition, and a more rational use of scarce local institutional capacities. Nonetheless, the validity and legitimacy of at least some of the heterodox critique is starting to filter through. Specifically, what has been acknowledged is the need to promote a better development of human resources and social infrastructure as well as pay greater attention to the debt problem. Unfortunately, suggestions and recommendations relating to these issues tend to be quite general and do not seem to modify substantially the core of the prototypical (conventional) SSAPs package.

An orthodox but more balanced appraisal of the need for complementary measures to reinforce adjustment policies is presented by Sahn *et al.* (1994) based on the CFNPP research programme covering ten sSA countries. This approach provides the beginning of a bridge (synthesis) between the orthodox and the heterodox approaches in recognising the necessity of supplementing and reinforcing adjustment measures with a set of critical complementary policies if sustainable long-term growth with poverty alleviation is to be achieved. They conclude that:

> while we have found that [adjustment policies] . . . usually do not harm the poor (and often benefit them), we are concerned nonetheless about the persistence of adjustment lending, and the lack of a broader vision about how to accelerate growth and alleviate poverty.

In their analysis they first point out that SSAPs were not meant at the outset to alleviate poverty *per se* but were instead designed to mitigate non-sustainable macroeconomic imbalances. Thus their impact must be assessed in this light. They believe that while faster and more stable economic growth will eventually contribute to an alleviation of poverty, immediate complementary actions are nonetheless necessary to meet the needs of the poor. Two types of activities have been delineated: *1)* transfers to raise income, such as food stamps, public works and income transfer programmes; and *2)* complementary investment to improve living standards and mitigate poverty: the building of social infrastructure and human capital and a physical infrastructure that can contribute to reducing transaction costs (particularly in marketing and transportation) and contribute to raising labour productivity.

This convergence of views based upon experience of the past will facilitate an understanding of future policies and the obstacles to their implementation, and thereby contribute to their success.

Notes

1. These results are based on the so called "income effect" of changes in the barter terms of trade between the two periods. This income effect was calculated by multiplying the ratio of exports of goods and non-factor services to GDP in 1987 by the percentage change in the average TT index between 1970-73 and 1980-86.

2. EIAL countries include Côte d'Ivoire, Ghana, Kenya, Madagascar, Malawi, Mauritania, Mauritius and Nigeria.

3. OAL countries include Burkina Faso, Burundi, Central African Republic, Congo, People's Republic of Guinea, Guinea-Bissau, Mali, Niger, Sierra Leone, Somalia, Sudan, Zaire and Zimbabwe.

4. NAL countries include Benin, Botswana, Cameroon, Ethiopia, Liberia and Rwanda.

5. According to the World Bank (1994):

    If Nigeria is excluded, the decline in the TT caused GDP to drop 5.4 percentage points between 1971-73 and 1981-86, but the increase in external transfers meant an increase in GDP of 2.7 percentage points . . . Adding these two effects, the total income loss between [the above two periods] was 2.7 percent of GDP, or 0.3 percentage points a year. From this perspective, the external environment was not much different in the mid-1980s from what it had been 15 years before (and for oil exporters, the external environment was better).

6. This drawback is also common to the two other approaches presented above.

7. Both studies include some non-sSA countries in their sample. In Elbadawi's case his sample consists of 31 sSA out of 41 and the Corbo-Rojas case includes 32 sSA out of 77 developing countries.

8. An indication of the relatively tenuous nature of the results comes through from the following quote from the *Economist* (March 5, 1994) referring to Elbadawi *et al.* (1992) study

    National statistics on Africa are usually wrong, out of date or both. A World Bank econometrician published a study in 1992 called: "Why Structural Adjustment has not Succeeded in sub-Saharan Africa". The Bank retrieved it from the printers, re-issued it with a less controversial title and pointed out that the analysis was anyway flawed: it failed to distinguish countries that merely signed up to a reform programme from those that carried such a programme out (p. 22).

Clearly, the World Bank did not appreciate or condone the original title!

9.   It is perhaps revealing that Stewart (1991, p. 1849) dismisses the counterfactual approach in dealing with the effects on human conditions, "since it is actual developments which are significant." As Demery (1993, p. 9) pointed out, however, "if alternative approaches produce less favourable welfare outcomes, this surely must be taken into account in seeking solutions to social problems".

10. See for instance the discussion in Fischer (1991).

11. See for instance Cornia (1991), Stewart (1992), and Demery (1993). Cornia reported that between 1980 and 1989, 241 SSAPs were negotiated in 36 sSA countries, of which 35 countries experienced about 7 SSAPs and 11 countries negotiated 10 or more SSAPs. Only very few sSA countries such as Burkina Faso, Rwanda, Angola, Botswana, Djibouti and Comoros did not have a programme in place over that period. Furthermore, Burkina Faso which had its own "self-adjustment" programme in place from 1983-89, finally negotiated an "orthodox" adjustment programme in 1990.

12. The above categorisation — although useful as a starting point — needs to be qualified. Expenditure switching policies and demand-restraining measures (e.g. fiscal discipline and sound wage policies) have to be maintained in the long run and are, therefore, critical to long-term growth.

13. The World Bank justifies reforms supported by SAL as measures intended to affect the balance of payments and public sector finances, and are expected to contribute to reducing over the medium term the macro imbalances that created the need for BOP support loans. On the other hand, SECAL may emphasise longer-run attempts at improving economic efficiency or the effectiveness of government programmes in the particular sectors.

14. Additional resources were also made available through the IMF: the Structural Adjustment Facility (SAF) in 1986 and the Enhanced Structural Adjustment Facility (ESAF) in 1988, in addition to the traditional IMF Stand-By Agreement (SBA) and Extended Fund Facility (EFF).

15.   This list of measures and policy areas is not meant to be exhaustive. The energy sector, for instance, is excluded.

16. In a review of conditions attached to a SAL received by Senegal, it was found that out of a total of 77 conditions, 13 called for studies and 30 could be classified as "preconditions" in the sense that they called for the formulation of action programmes, government announcements, "administrative strengthening", reviews and plans of actions. Clearly "studies" and "preconditions" do not, by themselves, alter in any way the existing policy and institutional status quo.

17. Notice that Cornia is not immune to the confusion between policy measures and outcomes.

18. Although the World Bank acknowledged that external factors (particularly external transfers) played a role in explaining growth performance, their relative contribution was much smaller, or less determining, than policy changes.

19. The reference period (1980-81) is not the most representative one for purposes of comparison.

20. Mauritania and Guinea were excluded for, respectively, not having major export crops and lack of data.

21. Burundi, the Gambia, Malawi, Niger, Uganda and Zimbabwe were classified as "mixed" marketing and "fair" exchange-rate performers. The World Bank had to conclude that, although sSA made progress improving incentives to farmers and limiting government intervention, no African country has yet adopted a generally sound set of agricultural policies.

22. Incidentally, total factor productivity is defined as the difference in the growth rate of real product and the growth rate of real factor input. Therefore, a positive growth rate of TFP means that resources are used more efficiently in agriculture but not necessarily that total real output actually increased.

23. This may also be related to the fact that the domestic demand for manufactured goods, stimulated through favourable terms of trade in some countries and easy borrowing in the pre-1980 period, was and still remains the main source of manufacturing growth in sSA relative to other developing countries. For the particular case of Côte d'Ivoire, see Koné (1993).

24. The World Bank also uses supplementary evidence based on international cross-sectional econometric equations linking different performance indicators to a variety of explanatory variables including policy variables.

25. A CGE model of Côte d'Ivoire built under the auspices of the OECD Development Centre reached essentially the same conclusion. A set of simulations of exchange-rate depreciation resulted in "a strong revival of the economy accompanied by a reduction in inequality and in poverty" (Schneider *et al.*, 1992; see also Lambert, Schneider and Suwa, 1991).

26. Professional reviewers of UNICEF's book, *Adjustment with a Human Face* (Cornia, Jolly, Stewart, 1987) tended to be critical. For example, Behrman (1988) characterises it as "a set of studies that seems to lead to the conclusion of little, or at least unproven, systematic impact of recession and economic adjustment on health and nutrition is summarised as finding that adjustment policy usually multiplies negative recessionary impact on the poor and vulnerable."

References

BEHRMAN, J. (1988), "The Impact of Economic Adjustment Programs", *in Health, Nutrition, and Economic Crisis: Approaches to Policy in the Third World*, House, Auburn.

BERG, E., G. HUNTER, T. LENAGHAN and M. RILEY (1994), "Trends in Living Standards in Latin America and Africa in the 1980s", *in* UNICEF, *Myths and Statistical Realities*, Draft for USAID, Comments, Development Alternative Inc., June.

BEVAN, D., P. COLLIER and J.W. GUNNING (1992), "Nigerian Economic Policy and Performance: 1981-92", Center for the Study of African Economies, University of Oxford, May.

BHADURI, A. (1993), "Alternative Development Strategies and the Rural Sector", *in* Singh, A. and H. Tabatabai, eds., *Economic Crisis and Third World Agriculture*, ILO, Cambridge University Press, New York.

BLOCK, S. A., (1994), "A New View of Agricultural Productivity in Sub-Saharan Africa", *American Journal of Agricultural Economics,* No. 76, Vol. 3, August.

BOURGUIGNON, F. and C. MORRISSON (1992), *Adjustment and Equity in Developing Countries*, OECD Development Centre, Paris.

CHEN, S., G. DATT and M. RAVALLION (1993), "Is Poverty Increasing in the Developing World?", Policy Research Working Papers, Working Paper Series No. 1146, World Bank, June.

CORBO, V. and P. ROJAS (1991), "Country Performance and Effectiveness of World Bank-Supported Adjustment Programs", PRE Working Paper Series No. 623, World Bank, March.

CORNIA, G.A., R. JOLLY and F. STEWART (1987), *Adjustment with a Human Face: Protecting the Vulnerable and Promoting Growth*, Vol. I, a study by UNICEF, Clarendon Press, Oxford.

CORNIA, G.A. (1991), "Is Adjustment Conducive to Long-term Development? The Case of Africa in the 1980s", Centro Studi Luca d'Agliano, Development Studies Working Papers, October.

CORNIA, G.A., R. van der HOEVEN and D. LALL (1992), "The Supply Side: Changing Production Structures and Accelerating Growth", *in*: Cornia, G.A., R. van der Hoeven and T. Mkandawire, eds., *Africa's Recovery in the 1990s: From Stagnation and Adjustment to Human Development,* St. Martin's Press, New York.

DEMERY, L. (1993), "Structural Adjustment: Its Origins, Rationale and Achievements", World Bank, Washington, D.C., June.

DOROSH, P.A. and D. E. SAHN (1993), "A General Equilibrium Analysis of the Effect of Macroeconomic Adjustment on Poverty in Africa", Cornell Food and Nutrition Policy Program Working Paper 39, Cornell University, Ithaca, N.Y.

EASTERLY, W. and R. LEVINE (1993), "Is Africa Different? Evidence from Growth Regressions", Draft, World Bank, Policy Research Department, Washington, D.C.

The *Economist* (1994), "Africa: A Flicker of Light", March 5, pp. 21-24.

ELBADAWI, I.A. (1992), "Have World Bank-Supported Adjustment Programs Improved Economic Performance in SubSaharan Africa?", Country Economics Department, Working Paper Series No. 1001, World Bank, October.

ELBADAWI, I.A., D. GHURA and J. UWUJARE (1992), "World Bank Adjustment Lending and Economic Performance in SubSaharan Africa in the 1980s", World Bank Country Economics Department, Working Paper No. 1000, World Bank, Washington, D.C.

GUILLAUMONT, P. and S. GUILLAUMONT (1991), *Ajustement structurel, ajustement informel : le cas du Niger*, Éditions L'Harmattan, Paris.

HUSAIN, I. (1993), "Trade, Aid, and Investment in SubSaharan Africa", Policy Research Working Paper No. 1214, The World Bank, Washington, D.C.

JAMAL, V. (1988), "The Vanishing Rural-Urban Gap in SubSaharan Africa", *International Labour Review*, No. 127, Vol. 3.

JAMAL, V. and J. WEEKS (1993), *Africa Misunderstood or Whatever Happened to the Rural-Urban Gap?*, ILO, Macmillan, London.

JESPERSEN, E. (1992), "External Shocks, Adjustment Policies and Economic and Social Performance", *in* G.A. Cornia, R. van der Hoeven, and T. Mkandawire, eds., *Africa's Recovery in the 1990s: from Stagnation and Adjustment to Human Development*, St. Martin's Press, New York.

KONE, S. (1993), *Sources of Growth and Structural Change and the Determinants of Exports: The Manufacturing Sector and Sub-sectors in Côte d'Ivoire*, PhD dissertation, Cornell University, Ithaca, N.Y., January.

LALL, S. (1990), "Education, Skills and Industrial Development in the Structural Transformation of Africa", Innocenti Occasional Papers No. 3, July.

LAMBERT, S., H. SCHNEIDER and A. SUWA (1991), "Adjustment and Equity in Côte d'Ivoire: 1980-86", *World Development*, No. 19, Vol. 11, November.

MKANDAWIRE, T. (1989), "Structural Adjustment and Agrarian Crisis in Africa: A Research Agenda", Codesria Working Paper 2-89, Dakar.

MOSLEY, P., J. HARRIGAN and J. TOYE (1991), *AID and Power: The World Bank and Policy-Based Lending*, Volume I, Routledge, London.

MOSLEY, P. and J. WEEKS (1993), "Has Recovery Begun? Africa's Adjustment in the 1980's Revisited", *World Development*, No. 21, Vol. 10.

SAHN, D.E., P. DOROSH and S. YOUNGER (1994), "Economic Reform in Africa: A Foundation for Poverty Alleviation", Preliminary draft, Cornell Food and Nutrition Policy Program, Cornell University, Ithaca, N.Y., July.

SCHNEIDER, H. with W. WEEKES-VAGLIANI, P. GROPPO, S. LAMBERT, A. SUWA and N. NGUYEN TINH (1992), *Adjustment and Equity in Côte d'Ivoire*, Development Centre Studies, OECD, Paris.

SINGH, A. and H. TABATABAI (1993), *Economic Crisis and Third World Agriculture*, Cambridge University Press, New York.

STEWART, F. (1991), "The Many Faces of Adjustment", *World Development*, Vol. 19, No. 12.

STEWART, F. (1992), "Are Short-term Policies Consistent with Long-term Development Needs in Africa?", *in* G.A. Cornia, R. van der Hoeven and T. Mkandawire, eds., *Africa's Recovery in the 1990s: From Stagnation and Adjustment to Human Development*, St. Martin's Press, New York.

THOMAS, V., A. CHHIBBER, M. DAILAMI and J. DE MELO, eds. (1991), *Restructuring Economies in Distress: Policy Reform and the World Bank*, Oxford University Press, New York.

THORBECKE, E. (1988), "The Impact of Stabilization and Structural Adjustment Measures and Reforms on Agriculture and Equity", Chapter 3 *in* E. Berg, ed., *Policy Reform and Equity*, ICS Press, San Francisco.

TYBOUT, J.R. (1991), "Industrial Performance: Some Stylized Facts," *in* V. Thomas, Chhibber, Dailami and de Melo, eds., *Restructuring Economies in Distress: Policy Reform and the World Bank*, Oxford University Press, New York.

WORLD BANK (1993), *Investing in Health,* World Development Report, World Bank, Washington, D.C.

WORLD BANK (1994), *Adjustment in Africa: Reforms, Results, and the Road Ahead*, Oxford University Press, New York, N.Y.

WORLD BANK and United Nations Development Program (UNDP) (1989), *Africa's Adjustment and Growth in the 1980s*, World Bank and UNDP, Washington, D.C. and New York.

Chapter 2

Sub-Saharan Africa: Its Prospects for Growth

Jeffrey C. Fine

The Global Environment

For Africans, the prospects for growth over the medium term, as assessed recently by the World Bank, are sobering (World Bank, 1994). Growth between 1994 and 2003 will average 4.8 per cent per annum for all developing countries, with East and South Asia expanding most rapidly at 7.6 per cent annually. GDP in sub-Saharan Africa, on the other hand, is projected to grow at only 3.9 per cent per annum. Though this rate is admittedly more than twice that of the past two years, given the average annual increase in population in most African countries, it translates into only about 1 per cent annually in terms of GDP per capita. Indeed, by the end of this ten-year period, much of the region's population will have an income comparable to that first attained in 1980, almost a quarter of a century earlier. Most disconcerting is the Bank's conclusion that the *proportion* of Africans in absolute poverty — already a disturbingly high percentage — will have *increased* during this period. Finally, these very depressing figures, it should be stressed, are based on the World Bank's most *optimistic* scenario, predicated on a benign global economic environment centring around five principal conditions: renewed growth; low interest rates; significant inflows of capital to developing countries; no further decline in commodity prices; and accelerated growth in world trade following the successful conclusion of the Uruguay Round. Clearly the projection is based on tenuous grounds, given the imponderable nature of global security as well as the profound political and economic change in the former Soviet Union (see Table 2.1).

Whilst the importance of these conditions will differ among countries in sSA, a number of comments can be offered concerning their overall significance for the region.

Table 2.1. **Global projections of growth and economic conditions, 1994 to 2003**

Indicator or region	1974-80	1981-90	1991-93	1994-2003 forecast	1994-2003 low case
Real GDP in G7	3.3	3.2	1.2	2.7	
Inflation in G7	10.0	4.6	3.3	2.7	
World trade	5.4	4.9	3.3	5.9	
Nominal 6-month LIBOR	9.5	10.0	4.5	5.8	
GDP	1974-80	1981-90	1991-93	1994-2003 forecast	1994-2003 low case
All LDCs	3.4		0.9	4.8	3.6
sSA	2.1		1.7	3.9	2.4
Middle East & North Africa	0.9		3.0	3.8	3.2
Europe & Central Asia	3.1		-9.8	2.7	1.5
South Asia	5.0		3.5	5.3	4.2
East Asia	7.3		8.3	7.6	7.1
Latin America & Caribbean	2.5		3.2	3.4	0.8

Source: World Bank, 1994.

Renewed Global Economic Growth

The projected recovery in the G7 countries is important for sSA. First it will buoy up demand for exports. Secondly, renewed growth may reverse the current trend towards a reduction in overseas development assistance.

Low Real Interest Rates

Although much of sSA's very substantial stock of debt is held on highly concessional terms, low real interest rates are important for new borrowing by the public sector and increasingly, the private sector as well.

Capital Flows

The presumption that private capital flows to developing countries will continue at the high levels of the early 1980s may be overoptimistic (Katseli, 1992). Furthermore, over 75 per cent of this flow has centred on 10 Least Developed Countries (LDCs), of which only one, Nigeria, is African. Nonetheless, given the tiny size of most African economies, even a small proportion of this flow could prove significant in alleviating an ominous shortfall in financing. Clearly, lower costs, higher returns and confidence in the soundness and continuity of public policies will be important in inducing more portfolio and private foreign direct investment in African economies.

Commodity Prices

Trends in commodity prices are significant for virtually all African economies, characterised by a high degree of openness to the world economy, inflexibility due to low productivity, poor infrastructure and overdependence on a limited number of primary product exports. In addition to a direct impact on export earnings, commodity prices affect overall economic activity through a wide range of variables including personal income, consumption, saving and investment, as well as government revenues. Furthermore, *volatility* in prices as well as the levels themselves are critical (Elbadawi and Ndulu, 1994). Given the governments' dependence on income from indirect and trade-related taxes, and the limited instruments available to offset major changes in income from exports, trends in commodity prices will remain an abiding concern for Africans. Overall, no further decline in global commodity prices is projected. Whilst a drop in the prices of tea, coffee and cocoa may possibly result from a simultaneous increase in production, African countries as a group should be able to maintain and even expand earnings from these and other traditional exports as a first step towards diversification over the longer term.

World Trade

African countries should benefit from the accelerated growth in world trade expected from the successful conclusion of the Uruguay Round. A more significant effect will be felt through the reduced value of preferential access, in particular to the European Union because of a general lowering of tariff barriers. In southern Africa, countries with strong trade links with South Africa will benefit from the latter's progressive rationalisation and lowering of its protection structure as a consequence of its membership in GATT.

Stabilisation, Adjustment and Growth

In addition to prevalence of these benign global conditions, future prospects for growth in sSA over the medium term should be qualified further in terms of success in maintaining three important macroeconomic balances. The first of these is the fiscal deficit, in order to avoid the destabilising effects of inflation. Governments must continue to widen their tax base and constrain public expenditure. Nonetheless, their efforts will remain vulnerable to changes in global interest rates and volatility in world commodity markets. Secondly, a sound balance-of-payments profile should be sustained through the promotion of traditional and non-traditional exports, supplemented, where possible, by development assistance and foreign investment. Here as well, African governments remain exposed: an unusually high dependence on imported intermediate goods, which is the outcome of decades of misguided import-substitution policies, implies that any downswing in export earnings resulting in a contraction of imports, will be reflected by a drop in overall economic activity, with adverse consequences for the fiscal deficit. Finally, governments must guard against an appreciation of the real exchange rate arising from inflation or windfall gains in export earnings. Avoidance of major fluctuations in the nominal as well as real exchange rate is essential to deepen confidence in the government's exchange-rate policy. However, this task will prove a major challenge, given the thinness of this particular market as well as a more general exposure to the many conditions beyond the control of national policy makers.

More recent experience indicates that an incorrect sequencing of policies can lead to perverse results inimical to growth. In particular, premature liberalisation of the financial market, in conjunction with high real interest rates associated with a sharp reduction in the fiscal deficit, can induce inflows of financial capital. These in turn result in an appreciation of the real exchange rate. The net outcome is a situation in which both exports and private investment are discouraged.

Aside from success in stabilisation, future growth in most sSA countries is predicated on other reforms. Here we single out three areas that bear most directly on economic performance. The first includes trade policy where "reform" typically entails the conversion of non-tariff barriers into tariff equivalents; consistency in protection across industries, and fixing nominal tariffs at levels that will yield badly needed revenues, but not distort production. Among the challenges confronting policy makers will be deeply rooted corruption in customs-and-handling agencies, porous borders (that paradoxically become less important with reform of trade and exchange-rate regimes), and inevitable cries for protection from distressed industries.

The second significant economic-performance factor is an improved management of the government's own business. Downsizing of the public service, against formidable political pressure, may prove costly in the short term because of redundancy payments and the potential loss of the more motivated and skilled employees. More expenditure can be anticipated to improve material incentives for those who remain. Improved standards of performance will also require the introduction and application of new organisational structures, and procedures for employee assessment and promotion. Nonetheless, African governments must simultaneously maintain the supply of essential public goods, notably personal security, education, health and utilities.

The third is a continuing rationalisation of the government's own direct involvement in productive activities. On the one hand, this task will entail the divestiture of public enterprises, a demanding challenge in light of undeveloped financial markets and political sensitivity to prominent, non-African minorities. On the other, the enterprises remaining within the public domain must be streamlined, subjected to tighter regulation, and selectively challenged by competition from domestic and external sources. Both tasks will demand financial resources and technical skills over an extended period, which are beyond the current capabilities of many African governments.

These "institutional reforms", as one long-time observer has noted, have proven the least successful aspects of structural-adjustment programmes (Killick, 1990). The challenge will prove even more formidable over the next 10 years. Not least will be the burden of past failures. Governments must contend with the cost of failed investments in institutions and people, as well as in specific projects. Furthermore, there is the sheer weight of numbers. Population in most countries has at least doubled over the past 20 years; its structure implies a very high dependants-to-potential-labour-force ratio, which will be expanding at a rate higher than that of the population as a whole. In spite of highly concessional terms, Africa's stock of debt will be reflected in the significant share of export earnings that will have to be devoted to servicing it. Whilst development assistance cannot offer a long-term solution, these resources are essential for bridging gaps in government finance and export earnings during a period of economic recovery. Unfortunately, a major reversal in current downward trends in development assistance is unlikely. Moreover, aid in future will be encumbered with additional conditions pertaining to such international concerns as the environment and will be targeted towards particular concerns and groups high on the specific agendas of the various donors.

The Political Economy of Growth

Concern with stabilisation and structural adjustment could divert attention away from three other issues that will ultimately determine whether many African countries will in effect achieve sustainable growth in the future or are doomed to remain permanent wards of the international donor community. The first is whether African governments possess the necessary *credibility* to manage their economies soundly, a basic condition for longer-term growth. The second is whether those exercising power are in fact *committed* to economic reform. The third and most essential issue is the *integrity* of national institutions, commencing with the nation-state itself.

The efficacy of policy instruments ultimately depends on an accurate prediction of the behaviour of economic "agents", such as consumers, savers, and investors. Such behaviour is conditioned by the credence in the instruments themselves and, more importantly, the intentions of those applying these instruments. Not unexpectedly, many African governments must contend with the deeply implanted scepticism resulting from continued failure over more than two decades in stabilising the economy and generating sustained periods of economic growth. In many cases, economic actors have attempted to insulate themselves from government interventions. This tendency is borne out in recent research by Professor Benno Ndulu on the Tanzanian economy (Ndulu and Semboja, 1994). His findings suggest that recorded earnings from exports and net foreign assets are equivalent to only 40 per cent of recorded imports. Furthermore, this shortfall of 60 per cent cannot be associated with more recent events, since it has remained remarkably consistent over the past 20 years, during which there have been several significant shifts in government economic policies. Research on other African economies would no doubt reveal "gaps" of a similar magnitude. Even after making allowances for the over-invoicing of imports, especially during periods of administrative controls over foreign exchange and import licenses, the figures infer that a significant portion of the "formal" sector has not simply gone "underground", but has in effect unlinked itself from public surveillance.

In places where economic actors believe that the momentum of structural adjustment ultimately rests on external assistance, the latter rather than the government's own stated policies becomes the principal determinant of their behaviour, especially with respect to long-term investment, critical in turn to sustained growth. One such example is Ghana, where would-be investors monitor the flow and terms of external assistance, in particular that of the World Bank, as an indication of whether the current set of policies *and* policy makers are likely to be sustained. The net result may be the opposite of what is intended, insofar as external attempts to support the government's credibility may actually end up undermining it by inducing would-be investors to adopt a "wait and see" attitude. Given the considerable acumen and rational expectations evident among African producers and consumers, the latter may exhibit economically "perverse behaviour" as they anticipate and attempt to offset the likely impact of various policies.

Paradoxically, governments may attempt to restore their credibility by deliberately constraining their scope of action (Collier and Gunning, 1993; Rodrik, 1989). Among the domestic measures is a provision for greater autonomy to key institutions in staffing, remuneration and action. One such example is the establishment of "parastatals" in Ghana and Uganda for the collection of government revenues. Another, yet to be undertaken in any African country, would be a highly independent central bank. A parallel approach would entail the transfer of jurisdiction over key areas of public policy to an *external* agency in order to withstand domestic political pressures and provide greater assurance of declared intentions (Fine and Yeo, 1993). This approach is evident in the recent establishment of the *Union économique et monétaire ouest africaine* (UEMOA) combining the existing West African Monetary Union (UMOA) with the mandate on trade flows previously exercised by the now defunct West African Economic Community (CEAO). As envisaged in treaty and enabling agreements, member governments will be surrendering most of their jurisdiction over monetary, exchange, trade and fiscal policies to new supranational executive, legislative and judicial institutions that will enjoy their own independent sources of revenue and can act directly with considerable autonomy. The credibility of the new structures, curiously analogous to those of the European Union, will ultimately rest on France as the external financier and guarantor (European Commission, 1994).

Nonetheless, this new application of regional integration, as an instrument for buttressing the credibility of *national* policies, will still depend, as will internal institutional arrangements, on three conditions. The first is continuity in external support, which, judging from frequent changes in their own policy agendas and interests, is not assured. The second is the relative importance of the country in question.

Thus authorities in Zaire, Nigeria, or South Africa for example, would still retain considerable latitude in practice for independent action. The third is the commitment of those exercising power to policies that more likely than not, may prove politically harmful in the short and medium term.

The very formidable agenda of political and economic reforms outlined above would test the *commitment* of any group of politicians. For African leaders, the challenge is even more daunting, since the rewards themselves are long-term and subject to other conditions that are often unpredictable and entirely beyond their control. Furthermore, the gains in concrete terms are meagre. As noted earlier, the *more optimistic* scenario projects a restoration of living standards, in 10 years time, to those enjoyed in 1980 but with an increase in the *proportion* of the population living in abject poverty.

Even if conditions remain buoyant, there are substantive reasons for questioning the commitment of those in power to the reforms necessary for sustained growth. In essence, many of these reforms will undermine the basis on which power is currently exercised and retained. Examples of self-sacrifice by the political élite are rare, especially in circumstances where the purported benefits to the ruled are uncertain and meagre. The logic of state intervention in Africa, in which the political élites have concentrated and wielded economic power, typically in coercive ways, would certainly suggest the contrary (Herbst, 1990). Such élites have established webs of patron-client relations in which their support ultimately depends on the economic "rents" made possible through their control of the government apparatus. Their hold on political power would be weakened by economic reforms, which would eliminate these rents. These observations, made in Kenya and some neighbouring countries by Gordon (1990), draw on both theoretical knowledge and the incisive insights of a practitioner. Not surprisingly, measures affecting the liberalisation of trade and foreign exchange, as well as other areas offering similar opportunities for "rent seeking" behaviour, have proven among the most difficult to implement.

Political commitment to major economic reform has yet to be addressed in a consistent and sustained way. Until recently, political systems have worked well for African élites whose overriding aim has been the retention of power. The introduction of multi-party politics may simply exaggerate rent-seeking behaviour in ways inimical to fundamental reforms essential for economic growth. The fragility of the civil society in most African countries, and in particular the absence of a politically engaged and sizeable middle class, could lead to deep cleavages, running along tribal, sectarian and geographical lines, which would be manifested in the composition and behaviour of political parties, very much along lines displayed at independence, prior to the imposition of single-party or military rule. Heightened competition through the ballot box, together with the elimination of previous arrangements for amassing and distributing economic rents may simply induce a search for new openings to maintain deeply rooted and ubiquitous webs of patron-client relationships. These could include, for example, access to the duty-free zones now springing up in many countries, as well as preferential treatment for would-be investors. Civic order could be maintained through shifting alliances among many parties instead of the previous division of spoils by a single party behind closed doors. In sum, Africans are behaving prudently by treating commitment to reform by the governing élites with considerable scepticism.

Questions of credibility and commitment inevitably raise an issue that lies at the heart of future development prospects for the region, namely the very integrity of the state itself. At least five countries are currently suffering from a total collapse of civil authority; in a score of others, including the region's most populous and more economically advanced countries — i.e. Nigeria, Kenya and South Africa — tribal, sectarian and religious tensions potentially threaten the integrity of the state itself. Hence, any discussion of prospects for sustained development must consider whether citizens of a given polity are prepared to subordinate their affinities to a particular tribe, clan, religion, or racial group in the name of an attachment to the "nation". In this regard, we note that structural-adjustment programmes implicitly incorporate a normative view of the state. We shall proceed to examine this "model" in the context of African experiences with nation building.

In retrospect, adoption of the nation state may have been inevitable. Nonetheless, it is worth pondering on the possible emergence of a "generic" African version. In effect, this possibility was forestalled by the "scramble for Africa", which occurred at approximately the same time that Japan embarked on its modernisation in order to resist a similar encroachment by European powers. Instead, Westernised African élites, towards the end of the 19th century and in succeeding decades, tended to associate the establishment of sovereign nation states, based on the European model, with self-determination and decolonisation. Other models, derived from historical and cultural experiences, were never seriously considered.

Ironically, the only serious alternative model was introduced by a colonial power. Modelled on British policy in large sections of the Indian subcontinent, "indirect rule", whereby sovereign authority was exercised through traditional rulers and institutions, was established by Lord Lugard at the time of conquest into Uganda and northern Nigeria. The system, from the perspective of the colonisers, proved remarkably successful. Colonial authority was maintained with minimal force and very few expatriates. Government was cheap and paid for itself. The system appealed to liberals and conservatives alike: to the former because of its apparent accommodation to the ruled, and to the latter as a natural expression of traditional custom and institutions. Its collapse at independence offers instructive insights into the system of government associated with the nation-state, a concept introduced at a very late stage, often at the moment of departure by the colonial power. Traditional rulers, lacking formal education and a base within the sectors of the economy in the process of modernisation, found themselves at a disadvantage in competing for control of the state with the emerging élite, typically from other tribes and regions. This contest was ultimately settled by conflict, marked at various stages by a dismembering of the state itself.

Anticipation of the need to accommodate tribal and sectarian rivalries can be glimpsed in the visionary proposals, dating back to the last century, for African unity. By expanding the boundaries of the polity, even the largest groups would be forced, as less powerful minorities, to form alliances that would inevitably cut across sectarian, tribal and ethnic cleavages. A not dissimilar logic, born of two world wars, underpins the momentum behind closer European integration. Unfortunately, this vision was quickly replaced by organisations of which the principal function was to prop up fragile nation-states. Possibly the sole consensus among OAU members has been a commitment not to alter boundaries inherited from the colonial era, although these often bear no relation to the distribution of tribes and ethnic groups, and cut across centuries-old movements of commerce and people. Indeed, the continuing reluctance to comment upon, let alone intervene in the affairs of another African state may stem from fear of disintegration of fragile national structures that must still claim the loyalty of their supposed citizenry.

To establish the legitimacy of the state, Africans have preferred to borrow from elsewhere. Of particular note in the first two decades after independence has been African Socialism, the principal tenets of which were drawn from contemporaneous varieties of European social democracy or its Marxist-Leninist rival. Emphasis on largely non-existent "class conflict" allowed ruling élites to downplay — in the short term — cleavages along tribal and sectarian lines. Not unexpectedly, this construct has proven no more enduring than in the former Soviet bloc, with its much larger and more advanced industrial and manufacturing sectors. Unfortunately, African Socialism provided a rationale for concentrating economic power within the state, a policy that simultaneously expanded the base of support for the ruling élite. Closely associated with African Socialism was another imported doctrine, of "dependency", with intellectual roots in Latin America. The international economic order, it contended, was inherently inimical to developing countries. Industrialisation could only be achieved through import substitution led by the state. The theory of dependency has been discredited, not only by the collapse of state socialism, but the rapid growth of East and Southeast Asian countries taking full advantage of a supposedly hostile international environment. Ironically, dependency theory has left many African countries even more vulnerable to the vagaries of the international economy because import-substitution policies have bequeathed an industrial structure that is over-dependent on the imports of intermediate goods. Furthermore, by implicitly condoning the use of national institutions to feed the patronage systems of ruling élites, both doctrines have seriously weakened the integrity of the state itself.

Structural adjustment programmes are based on a normative model of the state. The model has never been fully articulated, but its principal features can be inferred from oblique references by the World Bank to a "Scandinavian model", especially in its 1989 perspective on African development (World Bank, 1989). The private sector bears principal responsibility for the creation of wealth. The state's principal economic functions are to create the appropriate "enabling environment" for the activities of the private sector, to produce and distribute essential public goods, to rectify market "failures", and to reduce major disparities in the distribution of income and wealth. Clearly, the appropriateness of this model — based on secure nation-states with long-established democratic traditions, deep and rich civil societies, and highly advanced economic structures — is questionable, especially since economic recession has subsequently prompted a major reassessment by Scandinavians themselves.

Wrestling simultaneously with nation building and economic development is not unique to sub-Saharan Africa. European thinkers such as Max Weber explored both halves of the relationship, namely the impact of the state on economic growth, and conversely, how economic development and technological change have shaped the institutions and processes of the state (Weber, 1920). Not surprisingly, many of these thinkers came from "Middle Europe", where strengthening of the state was viewed as a legitimate and progressive goal, and economic change often entailed a proactive role by government. This line of inquiry was abandoned, for possibly two reasons. The first was an attribution of two global conflicts to nationalism, especially its most virulent and racialist expression in Nazi Germany. The second was a fixation on class division and conflict, not only by socialists, but other social scientists as well, both in Europe and North America. More recent and formal treatment of the relationship between development and nation building, albeit lacking the rich detail and sweeping scale of Weber and his contemporaries, can be found in work based on institutional economics. It can offer illuminating insights into such important questions as the nurturing of professional ethos in systems based on patron-client relationships (Leonard, 1993) and, by extension, help derive a view of the state that is more reflective of the values and aspirations of the groups most likely to be found in the vanguard of modernisation and change.

Conclusion

The overall mood of this reflection on Africa's prospects for growth has been sombre. Nonetheless, it is worth recalling that in 1960 Singapore was considered an economic basket case and few observers would have predicted a buoyant future for a South Korea shattered by war, saddled by a corrupt and inept administration, and bereft of the industry and resources of the northern half of the country (Naya and McCleery, 1994). Seemingly hopeless situations can be reversed and, in this vein, the "constraints" discussed by this paper should be viewed as challenges rather than insurmountable obstacles.

The need to maintain a balanced historical perspective is suggested by the various attempts over the past three decades to locate the "key" to sustained growth in Africa. The initial emphasis on the accumulation of physical capital quickly gave way to investment in human resources, in particular in education and training, both as a reflection of postwar European and Japanese experiences and in response to low rates of return in more conventional expenditure on physical infrastructure. Subsequently, "human resources" was broadened to "basic human needs", encompassing an ambitious range of public goods. By the mid-1980s, it was becoming evident that these investments could not be sustained by faltering economies. Attention consequently switched to macroeconomic policy. Stabilisation in turn has prompted interest in more fundamental changes of economic institutions and processes.

Viewed from this perspective, the renewed interest in political economy is both inevitable and timely. Whereas the behaviour of the private sector was once considered a function of government actions, the roles are now being reversed. The success of public policies now hinges increasingly on whether they are credible to private economic agents. This credibility in turn is largely dependent on the perceived as well as the real commitment of the ruling élite to policies that would test the political mettle of any government. The challenge is heightened by the need to legitimise institutions and processes that have but shallow roots, if indeed any at all, in African soil. Ultimately, the responses must come from Africans themselves, in the form of renewed political institutions and governments worthy of the past sacrifices and resilient optimism of their citizens.

References

COLLIER, P. and J.W. GUNNING (1993), "Linkages Between Trade Policy and Regional Integration", Paper presented at AERC Workshop on Trade Liberalisation and Regional Integration, Nairobi, December.

ELBADAWI, I.A. and B. NDULU (1994), "Long-Term Development and Sustainable Growth in Sub-Saharan Africa", Paper presented to SAREC Colloquium on Growth Equity and Sustainable Development, Stockholm, 9-11 March.

EUROPEAN COMMISSION (1994), *Note de présentation du Traité de l'Union économique et monétaire ouest africaine*, February.

FINE, J. and S. YEO (1993), "Regional Integration in Sub-Saharan Africa: Dead End or a Fresh Start", Paper presented to AERC Meeting on Trade and Regional Integration, Nairobi, December.

GORDON, D. (1990), "The Political Economy of Economic Reform in Kenya", Paper prepared for the Center for Strategic and International Studies, Washington, D.C., November.

HERBST, J. (1990), "The Structural Adjustment of Politics in Africa", *World Development*, Vol 18, No. 7, pp. 949-958.

KATSELI, L.T. (1992), "Foreign Direct Investment and Trade Interlinkages in the 1990's: Experience and Prospects of Developing Countries", CEPR Discussion Paper Series No. 687, London, July.

KILLICK, A. (1990), *Explaining Africa's Post-Independence Development Experiences*, Overseas Development Institute, London.

LEONARD, D.K. (1993), "Structural Reform of the Veterinary Profession in Africa and the New Institutional Economics", *Development and Change*, Vol. 24, pp. 227-267.

NAYA, S and R. McCLEERY (1994), "Relevance of Asian Development Experiences to African Problems", International Center for Economic Growth, Occasional Papers No. 39, San Francisco.

NDULU, B.J. and J.J. SEMBOJA (1994), "Trade and Industrialization in Tanzania: a review of experience and issues", in Helleiner, G.K. (ed.), *Trade Policy and Industrialization in Turbulent Times*, Routledge, London.

RODRIK, D. (1989), "Credibility of Trade Reform — A Policy Maker's Guide", *The World Economy*, Vol. 12, No. 1, March, pp. 1-16.

WEBER, M. (1920), *General Economic History*, translated by F.H. Knight, Collier Books, New York, 1961.

WORLD BANK (1989), *Sub-Saharan Africa: From Crisis to Sustainable Growth*, Washington, D.C., November.

WORLD BANK (1994), *Global Economic Prospects and the Developing Countries*, Washington, D.C., April.

Chapter 3

Development Policy for Africa: A Research Agenda

Jean-Paul Azam[1]

Introduction

Reviving economic growth in sub-Saharan Africa (hereafter referred to as sSA) is the big challenge of the 1990s for policy-oriented development economists. The previous decade has been that of adjustment, and sSA countries have devoted most of their efforts to fighting major macroeconomic imbalances. The latter were inherited to a large extent from the previous decade, but were made even worse by the negative terms-of-trade shocks of the second half of the 1980s. Nevertheless, with few exceptions, the growth performance of most sSA countries is dismal. Out of the 32 sSA countries listed in the *World Development Report 1993* (World Bank, 1993) with a known average annual growth rate of per capita GDP over the period 1980-91 (not including those without such data), only 6 have a figure equal to or higher than 1 per cent, while 11 of them have a figure below -1 per cent. The exceptions are first the very small economies of Mauritius and Botswana, with per capita-GNP growth rates of 6.1 per cent and 5.6 per cent, respectively, followed by Chad, the postwar recovery of which resulted in an average per capita-GNP growth rate of 3.8 per cent. Among the relatively large economies of the continent, Burkina Faso (9.3 million inhabitants in 1991) appears as a champion with an average per capita-GNP growth rate of 1.2 per cent. Even the relatively slow growers of Asia have much better economic performances than most African countries. Bangladesh has 1.9 per cent, Nepal 2.1 per cent, Sri Lanka 2.5 per cent, etc. Philippines is the only exception, with a negative average per capita-income growth rate over the same period. Hence, understanding the slow growth of most African economies[2] is a major challenge to researchers.

The most striking fact about sSA economies is that they are exposed to various large shocks, and seem especially ill-equipped to cope with them. The occurrence of these shocks is rather difficult to predict, so that investing in these economies is extremely risky. Economic growth is basically determined by investment in physical or human capital, and the recent developments of economic theory have emphasised the importance of uncertainty in holding back investment. The option value of waiting is larger, the more uncertain is the future and the more likely is the passage of time to deliver additional information about the prospects of profitability of an investment project (Dixit, 1992; Pindyck, 1991). This uncertainty of returns to investment is relevant both to private foreign direct investment and to public aid, although the latter should be less sensitive to risk insofar as aid agencies are in a better position than national governments to diversify their risks. Hence, analysing the different types of risks, their impact on investment and growth, and the way they can be overcome, is the core of the research agenda proposed here.

Governance and Political Risk

Probably the most spectacular type of shock to sSA countries that has attracted the attention of the layman is civil war. The recent events in Rwanda made headlines everywhere and were massively reported on television, but the entire history of sSA since independence is full of examples of civil war, as in Nigeria in 1967, Ethiopia for about 30 years (de Waal, 1991), Uganda (Mutibwa, 1992), Chad, Angola, etc. These wars have had dismal consequences on the economies and destroyed a lot of physical and human capital. In a classic cross-country study, Barro (1991) has brought out the impact of political violence on growth. More recently, Nehru and Dareshwar (1994) have shown that the number of revolutions and coups is a significant variable, along with the human-capital stock, in an econometric explanation of the growth rate of total factor productivity in cross-country equations.

There are countries, such as Côte d'Ivoire, Kenya, Madagascar and Senegal, that have not experienced this kind of turmoil. However, it is useful to emphasise that even though Africa has had some examples of international wars, such as the Uganda-Tanzania war, civil wars are by far the most common form of collective violence on the continent. Hence, understanding some of the determinants of the probable breakout of a civil war would be an important input for devising a policy aimed at reducing one of the major risks borne by sSA countries, thereby restoring investor confidence. Neglecting to pursue domestic peace as part of government policy increases political risk and thus inflicts a strong negative externality on potential investors. Among African investment opportunities, investing in a peace-keeping policy might plausibly offer the best social rate of return.

Many of the determinants of civil wars fall outside the scope of economic analysis, and cannot be managed through economic policy. Tribalism and religious diversity are the most common factors that set off political violence in Africa, with or without foreign interference, while inequality and relative poverty, at least within ethnic or religious groups, seem to play a minor role. Another cause of internal conflict, not exclusive of tribalism and religious diversity, is the competition for the control of natural resources, like land in Rwanda (on several occasions), or oil in Nigeria (in 1967). Nevertheless, casual observation suggests that in the past some governments have pursued conscious peace-keeping policies, some of which have had noticeable impacts on public finance (Azam, 1995). In countries where the population is divided along a number of ethnic or religious lines, governments have to use a combination of repression and redistribution of wealth to prevent civil war from breaking out. The cost of repression includes, among other things, the development of military expenditure. Berthélemy, McNamara and Sen (1994) discuss the determinants of military expenditure in developing countries, and the resulting militarisation of some economies. Some of the relatively more successful sSA economies, such as Côte d'Ivoire, and to a lesser extent Kenya, have used redistribution much more than repression, although their populations are highly divided among different ethnic groups, maybe more so than other countries where civil strife has erupted. In Ethiopia, Rwanda or Uganda, for example, repression has been the mainstay of government policy, resulting in massive slaughters. Understanding what triggers civil strife in some countries, and what prevents it from happening in others is one of the main research topics advocated in this agenda. The Annex to this paper offers an extremely stylised framework showing how the outbreak of rebellion can be analysed with a choice-theoretic model.

Scope of Redistribution Policies

A very plausible assumption to test is that redistribution policies are a major ingredient in a peace-keeping policy. However, it seems that redistribution aiming at equalising incomes within ethnic or religious groups does not hit the target. Although fighting poverty and inequality are very important objectives of a proper development policy, and are prominently among the ethical reasons for countries from the North to spend money aiding countries of the South, they do not play a crucial political role. One of the causes of poverty in developing countries is precisely that poor groups do not matter much to the political life of the countries (Azam, 1994a). What seems to matter politically is redistribution among ethnic or religious groups, such as public investment in poor regions funded by taxation of the richer regions. A striking example of this strategy is offered by Côte d'Ivoire (Azam and Morrisson, 1994), where the cash-crop producers from the forest zone have been massively taxed (mainly through a stabilisation fund) in order to finance, among other things, some public investments in the poorer savannah zone. Similarly, redistribution among the élite of the various groups seems to matter more than anything that happens to the other members of the groups. The example of Kenya seems to support this view (Bates, 1989): during the Kenyatta era, leading politicians from the minority groups got access on favourable terms to some of the property purchased by the state from the departing expatriates. The political system does not exclude the leaders of the minority groups. For example, the current President, Daniel arap Moi is a member of the minority Kalenjin group, while the Kikuyus form the largest ethnic group. Although he faced an attempted coup by mostly Kikuyu airforce officers in 1980, he did not meet massive ethnic opposition. A particularly important method for redistributing wealth among groups, which is also especially difficult to observe, is the creation of rents through market distortions. Trade barriers, labour laws, etc. are common examples of this approach.

An educational policy aiming at establishing an educated élite made up of the most ambitious individuals from the various groups is also potentially a subtle way of performing this type of peace-keeping redistribution. Original ethnic ties can eventually become quite loose as these people progress in the urban sector (Azam and Morrisson, 1994). This is reflected in the well-known urban bias that inspired economic policies before the adjustment era (Braverman and Kanbur, 1987; Toye, 1992). In many peaceful sSA countries, education is the *sine qua non* for joining the ruling élite, and there is a well-known educational bias in rural-urban migrations. It follows that the relative neglect of agriculture in the economic policies of the first decades after independence is a testimony to the fact that the ethnic roots were becoming quite loose as the educated sons of the planters, as well as other educated people, were in fact focusing attention above all on themselves. Therefore, opening access to the education system to individuals from minority groups is a potentially important way of redistributing wealth and political power among groups. Conversely, denying access to the education system to the children of particular groups might result in exclusion and, eventually, in violence. Determining whether the urban bias of the early years was an effective protection against civil war, and whether its weakening during the adjustment era (Jamal and Weeks, 1994) led to more political violence is an open issue.

Superficially, this type of redistribution policy seems to run counter to the usual view of rent-seeking, according to which the government is in fact ruling the country with a view to extract as much rent as possible in favour of its own supporting group. In fact, one can draw up a typology of governments according to what they seek to maximise, under what constraints. This sort of taxonomical outline was provided by Findlay (1991), singling out the difference between a predatory government and a bureaucratic one, the former maximising the budget surplus that it can consume for its own utility while the latter maximises the level of public expenditure. This assumes quite unrealistically, however, that the government does not face any opposition. Azam (1995) went one step further, showing, in a theoretical framework, how government behaviour differs according to its conjecture regarding its potential opponent's behaviour: a simple-minded Cournot-Nash attitude rules out redistribution and leads to an emphasis on repression, whereas a Stackelberg-leader government is likely to use redistribution as part of its peace-keeping policy, to reduce the opponent's willingness to fight to obtain power. From a social point of view, the latter is undoubtedly preferable. From the government viewpoint, redistribution is in this case just a subtle way to remain in power, and has nothing to do with altruism.

A Suggested Approach

The proposed study should therefore focus on case studies that bring out the trade-off between repression and redistribution. For the sake of comparison, two types of countries should be selected for this analysis. First, one should look at countries that are a priori very likely to break up for ethnic or religious reasons, but have managed to avoid civil war. Although it is difficult to build proper counterfactuals showing convincingly that a given country would have fallen into domestic violence had the government pursued other policies, there are many cases about which most observers would agree to diagnose that a high risk of explosion was present. The examples of Côte d'Ivoire and of Kenya seem especially remarkable in this respect. The former contains four different ethnic groups encompassing more than 70 subgroups, among which widespread violence could have erupted under different circumstances. Northern people, belonging to the Mandé or to the Voltaic groups, are predominantly Muslim. Southern people, belonging to the Akan or the Krou groups, are predominantly Christian or animist. The northern savannah zone is poorer than the southern forest zone. Moreover, a lot of immigration has been taking place in Côte d'Ivoire, especially during the years of the "Ivorian miracle", in the two decades after independence. It is commonly estimated that 25 per cent of the population in the country, and 50 per cent in Abidjan, are of foreign origin. Therefore, the odds seem a priori biased against peace being maintained in this country. In the 1950s, before independence, Côte d'Ivoire was the scene of several violent, xenophobic outbreaks. Yet against all odds, it has turned out to be one of the most peaceful countries in the continent.

Similarly, Kenya has to cope with a potential rivalry between the most numerous ethnic group, the Kikuyu, and the other groups. While the first president of Kenya, Mzee Jomo Kenyatta, was a member of the Kikuyu group, his successor, Daniel arap Moi, is of the Kalenjin minority group. Nevertheless, inter-ethnic violence, which erupted from time to time, has been circumvented and has been limited to small, sporadic outbreaks. The attempted coup by Kikuyu military in 1982 illustrates this point (Sandbrook, 1985).

Neighbouring Uganda, which has been the stage of one of the worst civil wars on this continent, is a clear example of the second type of countries that should be selected for this study. Milton Obote and Idi Amin ruled this country in a very repressive way. Both belong to minority groups in the north of the country (Mutibwa, 1992). They crushed all opposition from the dominant Baganda in the south. The resulting battle turned what Winston Churchill called "the pearl of Africa" into a land of nightmares. Hence, comparing Kenya and Uganda is potentially a very fruitful exercise for bringing out the determinants of the choice between repression and redistribution as part of a policy for staying in power. Similarly, it could be interesting to compare Côte d'Ivoire to neighbouring Liberia, as these two countries have much in common, except for the outbreak of war. It does not seem likely, however, that the latter will be accessible to research in the near future, in which case Togo could be substituted to it.

Togo remained peaceful for a long period of time after independence, and was at one point nearly a success story. Nonetheless, violence eventually erupted, and the process that led to it is probably worth analysing.

The history of Nigeria offers an especially interesting ground for study because it offers an episode of civil war followed by a long period of peace, in a country where the population can be divided into three main ethnic groups: the Housa and Fulani in the north, the Ibo in the south-east, and the Yoruba in the south-west. The civil war that broke out in 1967 referred explicitly to regional redistribution issues. The discovery of oil is what prompted the secession and the birth of the Republic of Biafra, in the south-east of the country, in an attempt by the Ibos to avoid sharing out the cake with the other two ethnic groups. After the return of peace, inter-ethnic equilibrium was the centrepiece of Nigerian politics. A careful analysis of the built-in mechanisms of regional redistribution in Nigerian institutions would probably bring out a host of important lessons in designing a peace-keeping policy.

For a study such as this to be interesting, it would be necessary to analyse in detail the history of public expenditure and taxes with a view to establishing how much inter-ethnic or inter-regional redistribution took place and how much repression was practised. This would therefore probably require economists and political scientists to work jointly. Public investment is an especially visible way of redistributing wealth among groups when ethnic groups are closely identified with regions, which is often the case in Africa. An important factor is whether the ruler or the ruling party belongs to the numerically dominant ethnic or religious group, and is wholeheartedly supported by it, or whether it belongs to a minority group. It is a basic principle of political economy (Frey and Eichenberger, 1992) that the government is not likely to give special attention to its own group if the latter is not likely to overthrow it, and should rather try to purchase the support of potentially opposing groups. This is probably why Houphouët-Boigny's government in Côte d'Ivoire was able to impose heavy taxes on the coffee and cocoa farmers of the forest zone — the majority of whom belong to the former president's ethnic group, the Baoulé — in order to finance huge investment projects in the north, such as the controversial sugar plants (Azam and Morrisson, 1994). Hence, unconditional support by a strong ethnic group is probably a good thing for some types of African governments, as it provides them with an incentive to redistribute wealth to potential opposition groups. Whereas a weak government that is challenged within its own ethnic group, or a government that is supported by a minority group has a shorter planning horizon, and might indulge in more predatory behaviour. The recent events in Rwanda, however, show that unconditional support by the majority group is not enough to guarantee peace when the minority group is not large enough.

A major problem with such research is that a large part of redistribution is not performed through budgetary channels, thus escaping direct observation. Quite a lot of guesswork would therefore be necessary, with economic theory and indirect evidence as guides. Simulation models of the computable general equilibrium (CGE) type can be extremely useful for that purpose. Most distortions of the normal functioning of markets in developing countries have their roots in rent-seeking. Imposing import quotas or labour-market regulations, for example, is generally done not only for the declared purpose of serving some policy objectives, but also for the more discrete objective of generating and distributing rents. Similarly, the control of the credit market, as well as the imposition of a restricted foreign-exchange regime, may be used for channelling resources to privileged groups in an unobtrusive way. There is thus a major trade-off between the reduction of political risk by way of these roundabout methods of redistribution and the efficiency and growth potential of African economies.

The benefit to the government of redistributing wealth through these indirect methods is that it is difficult for the outside observer to determine who, precisely, benefits from the rent, so that the government cannot easily be accused of misappropriating public funds. Even external agencies like the IMF are fairly ill-equipped to determine and control this type of redistribution. On the contrary, any redistributed money that shows up in the budget can be expected to give away too much information and eventually to result in different kinds of controls being imposed on them, limiting government discretion. We shall return to the issue of rent-seeking below.

Other Sources of Political Uncertainty

Good governance cannot be reduced to the issue of maintaining peace, although this is probably of the utmost importance in Africa. Political uncertainty results as well from political instability, with recurrent cycles of dictatorship and democracy, for instance, as can be observed in some sSA countries. The case of Ghana in the first two decades of independence offers an interesting example of political instability, with alternating civilian and military regimes. The case of Nigeria since independence is another (Bevan, Collier and Gunning, 1992), including the latest coup by General Abacha.

Many African countries have recently embarked on a process of democratisation. This is true in various West African countries and, with potentially momentous implications for the whole continent, in South Africa. Democratisation opens new avenues for development policy, but also generates as well new constraints and a new type of uncertainty. Democracy may certainly be regarded as a good in its own right, and its development as an integral part of the goals of development policy (Azam, 1994c). It does, however, introduce new risks, as very little is known about the policies that will come out of the electoral process. The transition from a single-party regime to a multi-party system with political competition might result in many parties' being defined along ethnic lines, thus creating an obvious risk of tribal rivalry. Moreover, the adjustment decade was also the decade when the role of bureaucracy was trimmed down, after it had got out of hand in the second half of the 1970s, fuelled by the proceeds of the commodity booms of that period, which were massively captured by the governments (Bevan, Collier and Gunning, 1993). Democracy might simply put political influence back in the hands of the bureaucrats and other educated élites, who

75

are better able to seize the opportunities available in a more open society than, say, farmers or informal-sector entrepreneurs (Bates, 1989). This could end up restoring the urban bias of the previous decades, and giving a new impetus to the development of labour unions, with probable negative effects on the competitiveness of African firms. On the other hand, by creating competition, democracy may result in a "contestable political market", making bureaucratic power accountable to the people[3].

Although democracy certainly entails some economic costs, measured in terms of forgone output, its social evaluation should not be restricted to this. One can define the value of democracy by the amount of material welfare that the people are willing to give up in order to enjoy an increase in democracy (Azam, 1994c). Then one can argue that the marginal cost of democracy, measured in terms of foregone output, must be positive in a political-economic equilibrium, if its marginal value is strictly positive (Azam, 1994c). Otherwise, democracy could be developed further with a positive welfare effect. It is not, however, a perfect protection against political risk of the type discussed above. For example, democracy does not automatically ensure satisfactory protection of the interests of minority groups, which could eventually adopt a violent attitude if they were prevented by the majority from fully exercising their political and economic rights (Berthélemy, McNamara and Sen, 1994).

Other types of policy uncertainty can occur, irrespective of the political regime prevailing in the country under study. Among stable governments, one can find examples of policy U-turns, the possibility of which brings on a policy uncertainty of its own. One such example is provided by the cycles of trade liberalisation and restoration of controls in Kenya (Bevan, Collier and Gunning, 1991). In a different context, General Abacha of Nigeria is taking his economy back to the pre-1986 era by restoring exchange controls, reducing central-bank independence, forbidding the sale of foreign currency by the private sector, etc. This is another example of policy uncertainty entailed by political risk, as Abacha's government took power undemocratically. However, policy reversals can occur for different reasons.

Coping with External and Natural Shocks

Some policy U-turns are in fact a (bad) government response to external shocks. African economies have remained to a large extent dependent on a small number of primary export goods, which are sold in very volatile international markets, so terms-of-trade shocks, and the policy response that they entail, are very important sources of uncertainty in African economies. Two main solutions to this problem have been put forward in the literature. The first one is price stabilisation, either at the national or at the international level (Azam, 1992; Guillaumont, 1987). Stabilisation funds, however, have lost all credibility, having shown very clearly in the past that they were unable to stabilise producer prices in the aftermath of the large negative shocks of the 1980s, as they were in fact mainly used as off-budget channels to fund public expenditures. This leaves a second route as the only one that could buffer these economies from these shocks: export diversification.

Export Diversification

As most African economies are primary commodity exporters, diversification is widely regarded as implying mainly industrialisation. The early years of independence were devoted precisely to industrialisation, with a spectacular record of failures. In those days, governments typically relied on the public sector to develop industry, and mistakenly put the emphasis on heavy industry. Moreover, they favoured import substitution behind large protective barriers, and this did not turn out to be conducive to the competitiveness of African (public sector) firms. On the contrary, the latter became quite often just another method of redistributing wealth in an unobtrusive way, within a rent-seeking framework. So the emphasis nowadays must be put on private-sector industrialisation, on export diversification, and on efficient import substitution without trade barriers. Mauritius has shown how to use primary-commodity shocks to diversify the economy, as the proceeds from three sugar shocks played a large part in funding industrial expansion within an enabling policy framework.

Moreover, "new growth theories" have emphasised the positive externalities that can lead to increasing returns to scale in the industrial sector (Romer, 1986). How far the case of Mauritius lends support to this view is a debatable issue. There is thus a need to study the behaviour of private firms in Africa. Very little is really known about the way African firms behave in the different markets in which they act. Of particular interest is the analysis of the institutions that are relevant to firms, like labour contracts, access to credit, access to foreign exchange and international markets, etc. From a political-economy point of view, the relationship between private-sector firms and the state administrative system is a central issue. Private-sector firms are probably an easy prey for the rent-seeking activity of many state agents and other administrative authorities. This is again a difficult claim to establish on firm empirical grounds, but quite a lot of anecdotal and indirect evidence can be gathered about this. As rent-seeking is not coded by law, it is likely to evolve quite unexpectedly as circumstances change. This is an additional source of uncertainty for the firms. Furthermore, the private sector is not only a victim of rent-seeking, it is also an actor in it, as lobbying and other kinds of group pressures are often at the heart of the establishment of some kind of control.

The legal framework, and the system of contract enforcement, taxes and subsidies are potentially very important determinants of the environment of the firms. Similarly, the role of the government in crowding out the private sector from the formal credit market needs to be analysed. It can be argued that for many African firms the lack of finance is the main restriction on their expansion. Financial repression is one of the methods by which the banking sector gives the government priority in financing; this must be analysed as an integral part of the relationship between the government and private firms.

Various research programmes in this field are in progress. The OECD Development Centre ran a programme on "Micro-Enterprises and the Institutional Framework in Developing Countries" (Morrisson, Solignac Lecomte and Oudin, 1994), with case studies of Algeria, Ecuador, Jamaica, Niger, Thailand, Tunisia and Swaziland. The World Bank is currently conducting a related project called the Regional Programme for Enterprise Development (RPED), with case studies on Burundi, Cameroon, Côte d'Ivoire, Ghana, Kenya, Tanzania and Zimbabwe. Panel data on manufacturing firms are collected in these countries, which means that in the medium term interesting results could be available. This analysis must be complemented by a macroeconomic and political-economy study, in order to bring out a clear picture of the whole set of policy issues involved.

As mentioned earlier, the competitiveness of African firms could also be adversely affected by labour movements that might develop in the wake of democratisation, especially in urban contexts.

Trade Unions and Labour-Market Institutions

Very little is known about the labour market in most sSA countries. Some information on this type of issues can be collected by studying examples of sSA countries where the labour movement has been active for a long period. In Senegal, for example, the labour movement has been active since World War II (Cooper, 1990) and managed to resist various reforms in the 1980s (Chambas and Geourjon, 1992). Neither can the labour movement be said to be non-existent in Zimbabwe and some other southern African countries. Moreover, as usual in Africa, there are some underground institutions beside the formal ones. For example, in Senegal, the role of brotherhoods is of the utmost importance. Similarly, castes play a part in this country.

In French-speaking countries, there is generally a tradition of minimum-wage legislation, often with a distinction between the minimum wage applicable in agriculture, usually called the SMAG, and the minimum wage covering the other sectors, often called the SMIG. In English-speaking countries, the minimum wage does not play as important a part as in French-speaking countries. Nevertheless, this institution had noticeable effects in countries such as Kenya (Collier and Lal, 1986) and Zimbabwe (Fallon and Lucas, 1991). Although minimum-wage legislation has a bad reputation among economists, like any artificial price fixing, it is worth further examination in the light of current theoretical research. The main reason for this renewed interest is that economists have turned their attention away from a simple analysis of its effects on wages and employment to examining the institutions that determine its level. The minimum wage is not fixed exogenously, and its effects thus depend drastically on the bargaining process that leads to its determination. Therefore, the diversity of the roles it might play is extremely wide. A notable characteristic of the minimum-wage legislation in African countries is that it does not apply universally or, when it does, the degree of compliance differs drastically between the formal sector and the informal sector.

A classic analysis of the effect of a sectoral fixed wage rate is the Harris & Todaro model (Harris and Todaro, 1970), where it is assumed that there is an exogenously given high wage rate in the urban sector, while the rest of the economy has a flexible wage rate. They then show how unemployment plays a part in the migration equilibrium. In this case, the minimum wage is an obstacle to efficient diversification of the economy, as it holds back the development of the urban sector by maintaining the marginal productivity of labour in this sector above that of the rural sector. One may imagine many other ways by which the minimum wage can influence incomes and employment levels. For example, Tabellini and Rama (1994) have shown that minimum-wage legislation might be used by workers in one sector for improving their (expected) lot at the expense of the workers in the uncovered sectors. Hence, the minimum wage, as well as other labour-market institutions, might be studied within a general framework of rent-seeking analysis, or political economy of government policy.

The government may intervene in the labour market in a more positive way, by pursuing policies to enhance labour quality. Health and education are gaining importance in development-policy thinking thanks to the "new" growth theories.

Policies Promoting Human-Capital Accumulation

A recent study by Nehru and Dareshwar (1994), among others, has shown how human capital plays a crucial role in explaining growth. In particular, expansion of the industrial sector requires a strong development of the local human-capital stock. The relatively successful African economies, like Côte d'Ivoire and Kenya, accumulated human capital at a fast pace, at least during the first two decades after independence (Azam and Morrisson, 1994; Azam and Daubrée, forthcoming). They have followed two very different routes in this respect. While Côte d'Ivoire relied mainly on heavily subsidised education (Azam, 1993), Kenya pursued a different policy: the development of the public education sector was somewhat restricted while private education played a dominant role. A wave of associative activity, called the *harambee* movement, was in fact responsible for the massive accumulation of human capital that took place in Kenya. The government was to some extent taken by surprise and overwhelmed, but it did not try to repress this movement. Collier and Lal (1986) hypothesise that the minimum-wage policy was instrumental in creating the incentives for the private agents to accumulate human capital. As the minimum wage was climbing very fast during the first years of independence, education became the only door to modern-sector employment, and thus to joining the élite (Azam and Daubrée, forthcoming). Similarly, in Côte d'Ivoire, education became crucial for people to acquire a social status, in what has been called the "Republic of the Good Pupils" (Azam and Morrisson, 1994).

The OECD Development Centre recently ran a research programme on long-term economic growth in Africa (Kenya and Senegal), and some developing countries elsewhere (Azam and Daubrée, forthcoming; Berthélemy and Vourc'h, forthcoming). This was an attempt at using the "new" growth theories in a time-series framework, rather than under the more usual form of cross-country analysis, to shed some light on the growth experience of these countries. In particular, these studies confirmed the importance of the accumulation of human capital in the long run (Azam and Daubrée, forthcoming). Although they are fragile because of the quality and the quantity of the available data, these historical and econometric studies should be performed for many other countries in order to bring out the diversity of the growth paths of actual economies. Of special interest in this line of research is the issue of the relative role of the accumulation of physical capital and that of human capital. The role of the financial sector — the development of which was quite remarkable in Kenya after independence (Azam and Daubrée, forthcoming) — in mobilising savings and financing investment remains an important issue. However, the current situation in many sSA countries, where banks are sitting on a lot of excess liquidity, points to the existence of other constraints on investment and growth.

The accumulation of human capital has been subjected recently to two severe negative shocks in sSA, the fiercest of which is probably the outbreak of the AIDS epidemics. Kambou, Devarajan and Over (1992) have shown that this virus affects the educated population in Africa disproportionately. Hence, this is a natural shock that is adding to the uncertainty of investing in Africa, as human capital is highly complementary with physical productive capital (Azam, 1993). Therefore, devising policies to contain this disease in Africa will be important to the development policies the continent requires. African governments will most probably have to adopt a strategy of "precautionary" accumulation of human capital, as the disease reduces the expected rate of return on public investment in education by reducing the survival rate of educated people. Therefore, as the private expected returns to education are also likely to decrease because of this risk, more effort needs to be made to stimulate investment in human capital if African growth is to be seriously revived. Moreover, Becker, Murphy and Tamura (1990) have argued that there are externalities in the use of human capital such that the aggregate returns to this production factor display some economies of scale. If this hypothesis were confirmed by empirical research, it would add another argument in favour of making education policy a top priority in the policy agenda. Otherwise, the disease-induced reduction of African human capital could precipitate a cumulative outflow of educated Africans to Western countries.

The second shock to the path of human-capital accumulation in Africa came with structural adjustment. In many countries that had to reduce public expenditure for restoring macroeconomic stability, public investment and expenditure on education have been cut drastically, while current expenditure was, at least for awhile, cut to a lesser extent. Moreover, because of the urban bias alluded to above, the returns to human capital to a large extent consisted of rents resulting from various policy-induced distortions. For example, in Côte d'Ivoire, the taxation of coffee and cocoa, on the one hand, and the quantitative restrictions on imports of manufactured goods, on the other hand, were of the utmost importance for protecting the standards of living of the educated élite, mainly employed in the public sector and in import-substitution industries. These unhealthy incentives to invest in education were probably reduced drastically during the adjustment era. This raises the issue of the quality of the human capital that is produced by the education system. In Senegal, for instance, the system has produced a lot of bureaucrats with a classic education enjoying automatic recruitment in the civil service for a long period. This in turn produced an overstaffed modern sector, a large share of which was just exploiting rents generated by market distortions, with dismal consequences for productivity and competitiveness.

Many other distortions can be analysed similarly to bring out the discrete redistribution dimension of their adoption. For example, the classic topics of monetary and exchange-rate policies look different when they are put under the light of rent-seeking theory.

Inflation, Exchange Rates, and Policy Uncertainty

Among the sources of policy uncertainty that can slow growth down quite drastically, inflation is an emerging issue in sSA. Compared to Latin America, Africa was a land of price stability up to the mid-1980s. However, many sSA countries have seen their inflation rate increase substantially, and Nigeria, for example, has recently gone into the three-digit inflation rates. The franc zone countries, which used to have very low inflation rates, have recently devalued their currency by 50 per cent, a rate that announces a doubling of the price level over a period of two to three years.

The Role of the Inflation Tax

The modern theory of inflation is part of the more general theory of taxation and public economics. Increases in the price level work as a tax on cash balances held by the private sector, which the government levies by printing money. A major advantage of the inflation tax over the other taxes is that its administration cost is minimal. Moreover, by taxing all the agents that use money, this tax can be levied even on agents involved in the informal sector or in illegal activities at exactly the same rate as other people. It is thus equitable in the sense that it is difficult to evade. One could even argue that legal savings are easier to transfer into inflation-proof assets than black money, so that black marketeers are more exposed to the inflation tax than other agents.

The proximate determinant of the rate of inflation is the rate of depreciation of the local currency. The latter cannot be held fixed when the government budget deficit is large, and mainly funded by a fast growth of the money supply. In many sSA countries, governments tried to solve this problem by rationing foreign exchange on the official market. Unless the police are very efficient, this generally results in the emergence of a parallel market (Azam and Besley, 1989). Then the official market for foreign exchange needs to be supported by an inflow of foreign exchange, to be sold at a below-market price. Aid and government royalties from mining firms are usually the bulk of such an inflow (Azam, 1994b), but the implicit taxation of some exports, including that of agricultural products, is also a source of funds for the official market. Hence, given the government deficit, there is a trade-off between taxing exports, while maintaining a fixed official exchange rate, and taxing cash balances, by letting the exchange rate follow more or less the market equilibrium price. The chosen mix of inflation and exchange-rate overvaluation has an obvious bearing on the competitiveness of private-sector firms.

A Source of Uncertainty

Inflation is also a major indicator of the stance of macroeconomic policy. As Fischer (1993) puts it, "a government that is producing high inflation is a government that has lost control". Therefore, a high rate of inflation is a signal of policy uncertainty, and announces either that one or several attempts at curbing inflation are going to take place, or that the economy will eventually reach a state of crisis. Patinkin (1993) describes the "feeling of malaise" that results from a sliding currency. High inflation is not consistent with a fixed exchange rate, so that a flexible rate, or a system of managed floating are necessarily associated with high inflation. For a long period of time, the franc zone countries have managed to avoid inflation by maintaining a fixed exchange rate. This should not, however, be regarded as an unconditional argument in favour of fixed exchange rates. There is a big difference between a fixed exchange rate for a convertible currency, what the CFA franc (the currency of African franc zone members) was until recently, and still remains partly (except for bank notes), and a fixed rate for a non-convertible currency. The latter almost automatically entails the development of a black market, which in fact puts the economy in a regime where the marginal rate is flexible. Hence, in the recent past, African economies could be classified into two groups, the low-inflation and convertible-currency countries, and the higher-inflation and flexible-exchange-rate or inconvertible-currency ones. Nowadays, the pole of price stability that the franc zone countries were providing is under threat, after the devaluation of the CFA franc that took place in January 1994.

Low inflation requires in fact two ingredients, determined in a compatible way. First, a low budget deficit is necessary in order to avoid an excessive growth of the money supply to fund the fiscal imbalance. In standard macroeconomic textbooks, it is customary to distinguish between fiscal and monetary policies. This assumes, however, that the government can finance its deficit by borrowing. In most African countries, the government has lost any kind of creditworthiness, so that monetary financing is the most common outcome.

A low budget deficit is not enough for controlling inflation, as emphasised by a long tradition of models initiated by Sargent and Wallace (1973). A given budget deficit can generally give rise to two different steady-state inflation rates because of a Laffer-type of effect affecting the inflation tax. Hence, in a rational expectation framework, this case of multiple equilibria may lead to indeterminacy of the rate of inflation in the short run. What is required, in addition to a low budget deficit, is one or several nominal anchors (Bruno, 1991). The most natural anchor is the exchange rate in an economy that can neither fix its money supply, because of budget deficit and underdeveloped bond market, or control wage rates, because of a large informal sector. The credibility issue that is implied by the multiplicity of rational expectation equilibria in these models leads to a well-known problem, often discussed in the framework of European monetary integration (de Grauwe, 1992). Joining a monetary union with a credible reputation of monetary conservatism is one of the possible means of solving this problem, which was adopted in the past by the franc zone member countries.

However, a fixed exchange rate is only compatible in the long run with a small budget deficit, limited to the sustainable inflow of foreign savings. A compatible fiscal and exchange-rate policy is thus necessary for keeping inflation low, and thus, for avoiding a very important source of macroeconomic uncertainty. A compatible mix of exchange-rate and budget-deficit policies, which is the basis for macroeconomic stability, is thus a major ingredient of a growth-enhancing policy.

This creates a dilemma for developing countries. On the one hand, there is a need for the government to invest in infrastructure and education, while on the other hand, this might entail an increase in the deficit, and thus in the inflation rate. Hence, while public investment is generally regarded as beneficial to the economy, except when the government wastes the money in building "white elephants", it might result in low growth by increasing policy uncertainty through the resulting inflation.

A Suggested Approach

Although there are quite a number of cross-country studies of inflation and growth (e.g. Fischer, 1993), there remains a need to analyse this issue thoroughly in a time-series and historical perspective, within the framework of a long-run-growth type of study. We have already alluded to this type of research above. Of particular interest, in a quantitative and historical approach, is to identify the channels through which inflation is transmitted to the economy, and its effects on growth. Such a study would have to assess the trade-off between the positive effect of public investment on growth and the negative effect of the resulting inflation, for a given level of non-inflationary financing. Obviously, such a study could not be done on franc zone member countries, although this issue might become very relevant for them in the near future. Nigeria (recently) or Zaire (beside hyper-inflation episodes), for example, or Guinea-Bissau and Sierra Leone, among smaller economies, would provide interesting grounds for analysing the growth effects of high inflation in African economies. Their rates of inflation, largely over 55 per cent per annum, have definitely gone out of the range that Dornbusch and Fischer (1993) use for defining moderate inflation. Similarly, Ghana and Kenya have recently suffered from inflation rates higher than 40 per cent.

Having a small budget deficit and a stable exchange rate, together with a liberal trade regime, is the most reliable way for a country to avoid high inflation. This generally requires a state of tranquillity that is unknown in Africa. As these economies are subjected to the unpredictable shocks discussed above, these conditions can rarely be met, especially by the small countries. Therefore, some countries have adopted institutions for pooling the risks of external shocks. This is the essence of the franc zone, which has guaranteed to a large number of small- or medium-sized African economies a stable exchange rate and a convertible currency, with the help of the French treasury, thus avoiding the type of distress recourse to trade distortions when a shock occurs as in other African countries. As a result, these economies have achieved a degree of economic integration that is testified by the convergence of their inflation rates, by their cross-border migration flows, and by some convergence of their legal systems.

However, it does not seem that the creation of such regional institutions for integration is the only route for growth to propagate among neighbouring countries. Agglomeration effects of the type analysed by Krugman (1991) seem to be at work, even across borders.

Regional Propagation of Growth

One cannot avoid being struck by an effect of this kind in Southeast Asia. Malaysia, Thailand, and southern China have followed suit after the famous four "Tigers" (Hong Kong, South Korea, Singapore and Chinese Taipei) have shown the way to fast growth, in wave of increased prosperity. The same issue of regional propagation of growth arises in Africa, and might become highly topical in the near future.

The reopening of the South African economy to official inter-African trade and factor movements will probably entail the same type of benefits for its neighbouring countries. Southern Africa might become the main pole of African development in the medium term. This can be analysed by looking at the past, as it seems that quite a few of the advantages of being close to a healthy economy were already at work in Southern Africa, even during the days of the embargo.

A fair amount of information on the potential of this country to stimulate African development can be gathered by looking at the benefits that its neighbours seem to have gathered already from this proximity. In fact, most of the richest countries in sSA are to be found in southern Africa, as a glance at the attached map shows[4], and this suggests that some spill-over effects are at work. The countries have been classified in four classes of GNP per capita. The group of low-income countries, according to the World Bank definition, has been further split in two subgroups, those below and those above $1 per day. The darker the countries are shaded, the higher their GNP per capita. This visual effect would have been even more striking had data for 1994 been available, for the countries of the franc zone have clearly had a significant drop in their current dollar GNP per capita since the January 1994 devaluation[5]. There is a definite need for a closer analysis to identify the precise channels through which the South African economy seems to pull its neighbours upwards, taking into account the fact that most of these countries benefit from favourable endowments in natural resources. These channels are potentially direct investment in neighbouring countries, access to markets for goods, labour migrations resulting in important remittances, etc. The results of such an analysis could help us gain a better understanding of how the political risks this country is currently facing might affect the growth prospects of its neighbours. The most important democratisation process in the African continent at the moment is probably the movement of reforms in South Africa. The end of apartheid is without doubt a major political event for the whole continent, as the future of a large number of sSA countries depends on the events taking place there.

Many countries in this area used to send large numbers of temporary migrant workers to the South African mines. The resulting remittances provided these countries with a welcome easing of the foreign-exchange constraint. This was the case for Mozambique, for example, except for a few periods (Azam and Faucher, 1988). Similarly, Zimbabwe has attracted a lot of temporary migrant workers, especially before 1980. Moreover, a lot of South African direct investment has taken place in countries like Botswana, Comoros, Swaziland, etc. Hence, this whole region presents some degree of integration of factor markets, which plays plausibly an important part in the propagation of growth among them.

A similar type of effect is probably occurring in the goods market. By giving access to some economies of scale, goods-market integration in this region, even if it is very imperfect, has probably played a part in determining the relatively high standards of living that can be found there (see map). Therefore, southern Africa offers a unique testing ground for the new ideas on economic growth and regional integration in an African context (Rivera-Batiz and Romer, 1991). Such a study would result in important policy recommendations, and could help answer the following questions: Are specific institutions required for reaping the benefits of regional integration, or are free markets enough? Can regional institutions guarantee market integration? The existence of the SADCC in this region, to which the OECD Development Centre has already devoted some research effort, makes this an especially interesting study.

Per Capita GNP (Sub-Saharan Africa)

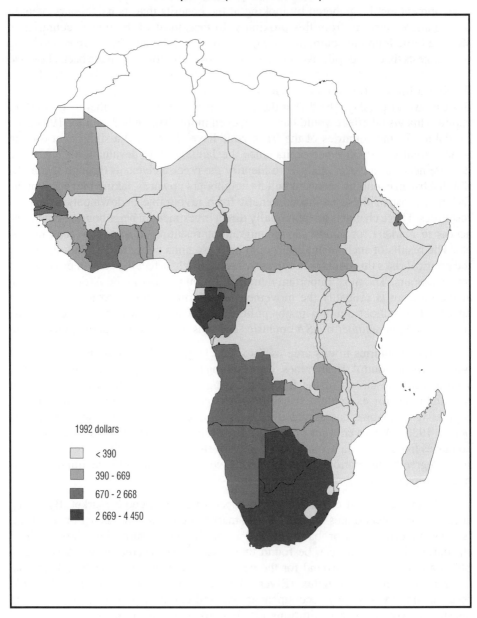

1992 dollars

▢	< 390
▨	390 - 669
▨	670 - 2 668
▨	2 669 - 4 450

Conclusion

This short research agenda cannot be regarded as definitive; it is meant on the contrary to set off a debate about relevant research topics on Africa for the near future. Many important topics, such as agricultural development, have been purposely left out, not because they are unimportant — on the contrary — but because they are or have been researched thoroughly, either at the Development Centre, or elsewhere. All the different themes alluded to in the present chapter have been cast within the framework of the relationship between growth and the various sources of uncertainty.

The first major research topic proposed here is that of civil wars and the policies that seem to be able to reduce their probability of occurring in any given country. The role of redistribution, either through the budget, or by the more discrete channels of distortion-induced rents has been put forward as a central issue in such an analysis, although there is just as much of a need to address others, such as the competition among groups for the control of natural resources.

The second type of research proposed focuses on industrialisation to promote efficient trade diversification as a defence against external risks. The study of the African private sector, with special emphasis on its relationships with the government, is central in this respect. Here again, rent-seeking is a crucial topic, as private firms are easy prey for administrative agents. Similarly, the role of labour-market institutions is crucial for determining the competitiveness of African firms, just as the policy of human-capital accumulation.

The third type of research advocated here is a long-run growth analysis for different countries. The aim of such a study would be to provide a testing ground for some important assumptions, which could result in important policy conclusions. Prominent among the issues to be addressed within such a framework are the effects of inflation and policy uncertainty, the effect of education policy, the positive externalities that industrial firms are producing, the effects of a regional propagation of growth waves, etc.

These are some of the issues that need to be addressed if we wish to understand the dismal growth performance of African economies, and if we want to contribute to the designing of policies capable of overcoming the obstacles that hold back growth in this continent.

A Predation-Rebellion Model

The aim of this appendix is to show that the issue of the probability of a civil war occurring in a given country can be subjected to the type of economic analysis that economists are accustomed to. The model presented is in the same vein as that in Azam, 1995.

The political economy of developing countries has not attracted as much attention from economists as that of industrialised economies. This is due, among other things, to the intellectual fascination for voting systems, which has been one of the mainstays of public choice theory but is not generally relevant for most developing countries. Many poor countries, especially in Africa, have no democratic institutions and are subject to some form of personal rule (Sandbrook, 1985). Findlay (1991) is one of the rare authors who has taken a few steps in the direction of a formal analysis of developing-country governments. He offers a taxonomic analysis of governments ranging from the bureaucratic state, which maximises public expenditures, to the predatory state, which maximises the surplus of resources over general expenditures for its own consumption. Although it is a stimulating approach, it should not be pushed too far, as we can regard a bureaucratic government as a special case of a predatory government which lets its own consumption appear in the budgetary books, while the normal predatory state gets the surplus out of the books before consuming it. Another important difference between the two is that the usual predatory state is run for the benefit of a smaller group than the bureaucratic state, which leaves something to be allocated to all bureaucrats. This may be regarded more as a difference in the intensity of predation, rather than as a deep qualitative difference. Hence, the predatory government may be regarded as the archetypical undemocratic government in developing countries. Nonetheless, although such a government is not directly accountable to the people through the ballot box, it generally has to face rebellion if it goes too far in extracting resources from the people. The present appendix aims at providing an extremely simple model of the interaction between predation and rebellion.

Let P be the "amount of predation" that the government extracts from the people. By "predation", we mean to emphasise that governments in the real world manage to capture resources from the people by a number of different means. Besides the usual taxes and compulsory services that it can get, there are many less visible means of acquiring resources, such as the inflation tax, currency overvaluation, import quotas, payment arrears to parastatals, etc.

Let R be the amount of rebellion that the people put up as a response to the government predation.

The main assumption of the model is that there is a political process in this economy such that the probability of the government's being overthrown is an increasing function of the amount of rebellion put up by the people. Call this probability $q(R)$, $q'(R) > 0$. It is natural to assume that this function has increasing returns to scale for small levels of rebellion. Figure A.1 illustrates a typical shape for this relationship. Define R^+ as the amount of rebellion such that $q'(R^+) = q(R^+)/R^+$. It is the value of R such that the tangent to $q(R)$ passes through the origin. It is the point that maximises the probability of overthrowing the government per unit of rebellion. It is not generally an equilibrium point of this model, but it is a useful benchmark.

Figure A.1.

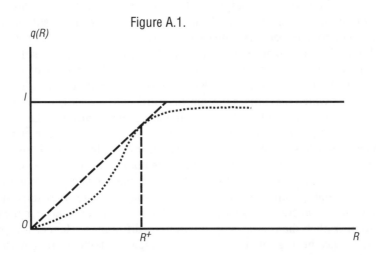

For the sake of simplicity, we assume that the utility function of the people is linear, which implies risk neutrality, and that its resource endowment Y is exogenous. Then, if the government is not overthrown, the representative private agent ("the people") gets a utility level $Y - P$, whereas if the government is overthrown, the people get Y. Moreover, we assume that any level of rebellion R inflicts on the people a per unit disutility level y. In a more developed model, y could be made a function of the government defence expenditures. Then, expected utility maximisation entails the following minimisation exercise:

$$\min_{R} \ (1-q(R))\,P + \gamma R.$$

(A.1)

The first-order condition for this problem can be written:

$$q'(R) \leq \gamma / P$$

(A.2)

Then, the decision rule of the people may be described by the following rebellion function, which displays a discontinuous jump at $P = P^+$, defined by $P^+ = \gamma / q'(R^+)$:

$$R^* = 0 \ if \ q'(R^+) \leq \gamma / P,$$
$$R^* = R^*(\gamma / P) \ if \ q'(R^+) > \gamma / P$$

(A.3)

It is represented in Figures A.2 and A.3 as the thick part of the horizontal axis, and the upwards sloping convex function for $P > P^+$. Then, its slope is given by:

$$\partial R^* / \partial P = -\gamma / q'' P^2$$

(A.4)

Figure A.2.

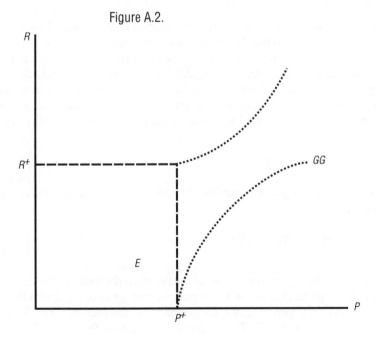

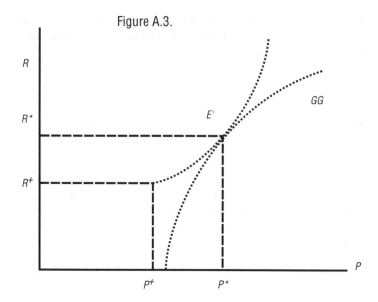

Figure A.3.

Notice, by examining Figure A.1 that the equilibrium cannot be found where $q'' > 0$, so that the derivative in (A.4) is necessarily positive along the upward sloping part of the $R^*(P)$ curve. Then, this curve is steeper, the larger is γ.

Now, there are two possible types of equilibria in this model. To show this in the simplest way, assume also that the utility function of the government is linear, so that it enjoys P if it stays in power, and nothing if it is overthrown. This is again equivalent to assuming risk-neutrality. Assume in addition that any level of rebellion R inflicts on the government a loss of utility of α. In a more elaborate version of this model, some expenditures by the government for staying in power could be taken into account (see Azam, 1995). Then, its problem is to maximise its expected utility G:

$$\max_{P} G \equiv (1 - q(R)) P - \alpha R.$$

(A.5)

The slope of the government indifference curves, marked GG on Figures A.2 and A.3 is given by:

$$\partial R / \partial P = (1 - q(R)) / (\alpha + q'(R)P)$$

(A.6)

It is flatter, the higher the degree of aversion to rebellion α, the higher P, or the closer R to R^+. Figures A.2 and A.3 illustrate the two types of equilibria that can show up in this model. In Figure A.2, the government indifference curve is flat enough for the preferred point to be E. This represents a "Limit-Predation Strategy": The government pushes the predatory behaviour up to the maximum point that may be reached without triggering any rebellion. This requires the $R^*(P)$ curve to be relatively steep, and the GG curve to be relatively flat. Moreover, it requires the function $q(R)$ to be flat enough to have R^+ relatively large. In other words, this equilibrium is more likely to prevail:

(i) the higher is the unit cost of rebellion (α and y) for the two actors,

(ii) the higher is the minimum rebellion required to reach decreasing returns to scale,

(iii) the more elastic is $q'(R)$, etc.

When these conditions do not hold, we may get the equilibrium depicted in Figure A.3. There, the equilibrium is such that $\{R^{**}, P^*\} > \{R^+, P^+\}$. This is a situation when there is rebellion, which prevails if none of the conditions expressed above holds. So, the rebellion is likely to be observed when the unit costs α and γ are relatively small, and when R^+ is small. It is a case where the government can be overthrown easily, and where both actors do not have a strong aversion to rebellion.

This very simple model is much too abstract to deliver much information on the real world. It does, however, bring out three important points to explain why some countries are rebellion prone, while others are peaceful:

(i) there is a positive upper bound on the amount of predation that the government can practice without triggering any rebellion,

(ii) rebellious activity is likely to be observed when the government is relatively weak, and

(iii) anything that makes the unit cost of rebellion higher for the government or the people increases the likelihood of no rebellion occurring.

We can discuss briefly the changes that would occur in these results by changing the model slightly. First, by lifting the risk-neutrality assumption for the people, one could make the equilibrium dependent on Y. In that case, the effect will depend on the degree of risk aversion. Similarly, by assuming risk aversion for the government, one could make the peaceful equilibrium more likely.

Notes

1. I would like to express my thanks to Jean-Claude Berthélemy for his very helpful comments and to Catherine Lefort who produced the map used in the final section of the paper. Suggestions from Patrick Guillaumont were also very useful. So many others contributed pertinent comments, that it would be impossible to name all of them here, but this in no way diminishes the author's gratitude towards them.

2. "Africa" and "African" in this chapter refer to sub-Saharan Africa.

3. I owe this idea to J.-C. Berthélemy.

4. I wish to thank Catherine Lefort for producing this map.

5. I owe this point to Patrick Guillaumont.

References

AZAM, J.-P. (1992), "Terms of Trade Fluctuations and Stabilisation of Producer Prices by Compensatory Taxation", *European Economic Review*, No. 36, pp. 101-118.

AZAM, J.-P. (1993), "The 'Côte d'Ivoire' Model of Endogenous Growth", *European Economic Review (Papers & Proceedings)*, No. 37, pp. 566-576.

AZAM, J.-P. (1994a), "The Uncertain Distributional Impact of Structural Adjustment in Sub-Saharan Africa", *in* R. van der Hooven and F. van der Kraaij, eds., *Structural Adjustment and Beyond in Sub-Saharan Africa*, pp. 100-113, DGIS-James Currey-Heinemann, The Hague.

AZAM, J.-P. (1994b), "Dollars en solde: politique de change et inflation au Nigéria (1980-1993)", Paper presented at the 1994 Annual Congress of the AFSE, Paris (published in *Revue économique*, no. 46, pp. 727-737, May 1995).

AZAM, J.-P. (1994c), "Democracy and Development: A Theoretical Framework", *Public Choice*, No. 80, pp. 293-305.

AZAM, J.-P. (forthcoming), "How to Pay for the Peace? A Theoretical Framework with References to African Countries", *Public Choice,* No. 83, pp. 173-184.

AZAM, J.-P. and T. BESLEY (1989), "General Equilibrium with Parallel Markets for Goods and Foreign Exchange: Theory and Application to Ghana", *World Development*, No. 17, pp. 1921-30.

AZAM, J.-P. and C. DAUBRÉE (forthcoming), *Contourner l'État: La croissance économique au Kenya (1964-1990)*, Development Centre, OECD, Paris.

AZAM, J.-P. and J.-J. FAUCHER (1988), "The Case of Mozambique", *in* J.C. Berthélemy, J.-P. Azam and J.-J. Faucher, eds., *The Supply of Manufactured Goods and Agricultural Development (The Case of Madagascar, The Case of Mozambique)*, Development Centre Papers, OECD, Paris.

AZAM, J.-P. and C. MORRISSON (1994), *The Political Feasibility of Adjustment in Côte d'Ivoire and Morocco*, Development Centre Studies, OECD, Paris.

BARRO, R. (1991), "Economic Growth in a Cross-section of Countries", *Quarterly Journal of Economics*, No. 106, pp. 407-441.

BATES, R.H. (1989), *Beyond the Miracle of the Market. The Political Economy of Agrarian Development in Kenya*, Cambridge University Press, Cambridge.

BECKER, G.S., K.M. MURPHY and R. TAMURA (1990), "Human Capital, Fertility and Economic Growth", *Journal of Political Economy*, No. 98, pp. S12-S37.

BERTHÉLEMY, J.-C., R. McNAMARA and S. SEN (1994), *The Disarmament Dividend: Challenges for Development Policy*, Policy Brief No. 8, Development Centre, OECD, Paris.

BERTHÉLEMY, J.-C. and A; VOURC'H (forthcoming), *La croissance économique au Sénégal depuis l'indépendance*, Development Centre, OECD, Paris.

BEVAN, D., P. COLLIER and J.W. GUNNING (1991), "The Macroeconomics of Kenyan Trade Liberalisation", Mimeo, Centre for the Study of African Economies, Oxford.

BEVAN, D., P. COLLIER and J.W. GUNNING (1992), *Nigeria, 1970-1990*, Country Study No. 11, International Centre for Economic Growth, ICS Press, San Francisco.

BEVAN, D., P. COLLIER and J.W. GUNNING (1993), "Trade Shocks in Developing Countries", *European Economic Review*, No. 37, pp. 557-565.

BRAVERMAN, A. and R. KANBUR (1987), "Urban Bias and the Political Economy of Agricultural Reform", *World Development*, No. 15, pp. 1179-1187.

BRUNO, M. (1991), *High Inflation and the Nominal Anchor of an Open Economy*, Essays in International Finance, No. 183, International Finance Section, Princeton.

CHAMBAS, G. and A.M. GEOURJON (1992), "The New Industrial Policy in Senegal: A Highly Controversial Reform", in R. Adhikari, C. Kirkpatrick and J. Weiss, eds., *Industrial and Trade Policy Reform in Developing Countries*, pp. 135-149, Manchester University Press, Manchester.

COLLIER, P., and D. LAL (1986), *Labour and Poverty in Kenya: 1900-1980*, Clarendon Press, Oxford.

COOPER, F. (1990), "The Senegalese General Strike of 1946 and the Labor Question in Post-War French Africa", *Canadian Journal of African Studies*, No. 24, pp. 165-215.

DE GRAUWE, P. (1992), *The Economics of Monetary Integration*, Oxford University Press, Oxford.

DE WAAL, A. (1991), *Evil Days: Thirty Years of War and Famine in Ethiopia*, An Africa Watch Report, New York.

DIXIT, A. (1992), "Investment and Hysteresis", *Journal of Economic Perspectives*, No. 6, pp. 107-132.

DORNBUSCH, R. and S. FISCHER (1993), "Moderate Inflation", *World Bank Economic Review*, No. 7, pp. 1-44.

FALLON, P.R. and R.E.B. LUCAS (1991), "The Impact of Changes in Job Security Regulations in India and Zimbabwe", *World Bank Economic Review*, No. 5, pp. 395-413.

FINDLAY, R. (1991), "The New Political Economy: Its Explanatory Power for LDCs", in G.M. Meier, ed., *Politics and Policy Making in Developing Countries*, pp. 13-40, ICEG, ICS Press, San Francisco.

FISCHER, S. (1993), "The Role of Macroeconomic Factors in Growth", *Journal of Monetary Economics*, No. 32, pp. 485-512.

FREY, B.S. and R. EICHENBERGER (1992), "The Political Economy of Stabilisation Programmes in Developing Countries", Technical Paper No. 59, Development Centre, OECD, Paris.

GUILLAUMONT, P. (1987), "From Export Instability Effects to International Stabilisation Policies", *World Development*, No. 15, pp. 633-643.

HARRIS, J.R. and M. TODARO (1970), "Migration, Unemployment and Development: A Two-Sector Analysis", *American Economic Review*, No. 60, pp.126-142.

JAMAL, V. and J. WEEKS (1994), *Africa Misunderstood, or Whatever Happened to the Rural-Urban Gap?*, MacMillan, London.

KAMBOU, G., S. DEVARAJAN and M. OVER (1992), "The Economic Impact of AIDS in an African Country: Simulations with a Computable General Equilibrium Model of Cameroon", *Journal of African Economies*, No. 1, pp. 109-130.

KRUGMAN, P. (1991), *Geography and Trade*, MIT Press, Cambridge, MA.

LAFAY, J.-D. and J. LECAILLON (1993), *The Political Dimension of Economic Adjustment*, Development Centre, OECD, Paris.

MORRISSON, C., J.D. LAFAY and S. DESSUS (1993), *La Faisabilité politique de l'ajustement dans les pays africains*, Document technique No. 88, Development Centre, OECD, Paris.

MORRISSON, C., J.D. LAFAY and S. DESSUS (1994), "The Political Conditions of Adjustment in Africa: 1980-1990", in R. van der Hooven and F. van der Kraaij, eds., *Structural Adjustment and Beyond in Sub-Saharan Africa*, pp. 126-148, DGIS-James Currey-Heinemann, The Hague.

MORRISSON, C., H.B. SOLIGNAC LECOMTE and X. OUDIN (1994), *Micro-Entreprises and the Institutional Framework in Developing Countries*, Development Centre Studies, OECD, Paris.

MUTIBWA, P. (1992), *Uganda Since Independence: A Story of Unfulfilled Hopes*, Hurst & Company, London.

NEHRU, V. and A. DARESHWAR (1994), "New Estimates of Total Factor Productivity Growth for Developing and Industrial Countries", Policy Research Working Paper 1313, The World Bank, Washington, D.C.

PATINKIN, D. (1993), "Israel's Stabilisation Program of 1985, Or Some Simple Truths of Monetary Theory", *Journal of Economic Perspectives*, No. 7, pp. 103-128.

PINDYCK, R.S. (1991), "Irreversibility, Uncertainty, and Investment", *Journal of Economic Literature*, No. 29, pp. 1110-1152.

RIVERA-BATIZ, L. and P. ROMER (1991), "Economic Integration and Endogenous Growth", *Quarterly Journal of Economics*, No. 56, pp. 531-555.

ROMER, P.M. (1986), "Increasing Returns and Long-Run Growth", *Journal of Political Economy*, No. 94, pp. 1002-1037.

SANDBROOK, R. (1985), *The Politics of Africa's Economic Stagnation*, Cambridge University Press, Cambridge.

SARGENT, T J. and N. WALLACE (1973), "Rational Expectations and the Dynamics of Hyperinflation", *International Economic Review*, No. 14, pp. 328-350.

TABELLINI, G. and M. RAMA (1994), "Endogenous Product and Labour Market Distortions", Labor Market Workshop, The World Bank, Washington, D.C.

TOYE, J. (1992), "Interest Group Politics and Implementation of Adjustment Policies in Sub-Saharan Africa", *Journal of International Development*, No. 4, pp. 183-197.

WORLD BANK (1993), *World Development Report*, The World Bank, Washington, D.C.

Chapter 4

Experiences and Lessons from Research in Tanzania

Alexander H. Sarris

Introduction

The objective of this short paper is to utilise research experience in Tanzania over the four year period 1989-1993, in the course of co-ordinating a large study, in order to draw more general lessons about research methodology and useful research areas in sub-Saharan Africa (sSA).

The research problem that was the objective of the study was to examine the impact of stabilisation and structural adjustment programmes (SSAPs) on the welfare of households and especially poor households. This is a problem that has been the object of much heated debate in recent years within African circles and among donors, especially after UNICEF's attack on SSAPs (Cornia *et al.*, 1987). The Tanzania project was part of a much larger multi-country and multi-year project to investigate this problem in several sub-Saharan Africa countries, which was funded by USAID and conducted by the Cornell University Food and Nutrition Policy Program. Many sSA governments used the issue as an excuse to not adjust or apply corrective domestic policies. Tanzania was one of the fiercest resisters to SSAPs, and the alleged adverse impacts on the poor was one of the major arguments used against instituting reforms. Nevertheless, the debate concerning SSAPs and their impact on the poor in Tanzania was quite confused because there was very little analytical or empirical basis on which to base opinion.

Tanzania is one of the poorest countries in the world. After a protracted period of crisis in the late 1970s and early 1980s, the government began implementing in 1984, but mainly in 1986, successive SSAPs. Until the early 1990s, the conventional wisdom in Tanzania, shared by most policy makers and analysts, was that the real incomes of households had declined considerably during the late 1970s and early 1980s. After the onset of adjustment, the declining real income trend had stopped, and in fact there had been some improvement in the early 1990s. Nevertheless, real incomes at the end of the 1980s or early 1990s were thought to be considerably below those of the 1970s, and poverty was considered to have increased. These beliefs were supported by trends in official GDP statistics, which showed that real per capita GDP had declined by 12 per cent between 1976 and 1984, while rising by 7 per cent between 1984 and 1991. They were also supported by some micro studies (e.g. Bevan *et al.*, 1988).

In the sequel, the methodological issues in dealing with the problem at hand are outlined, the various results obtained are highlighted, and areas where it is felt that improvements in knowledge through more research would have a high pay-off in terms of better information for policy making are pointed out.

Methodological Issues

Stabilisation and adjustment in the past have been regarded mostly as macro issues. However, poverty and the welfare of households are generally regarded and examined as micro issues. Hence, in order to examine the consequences of largely macro policies on household welfare, one needs a methodology to go from macro to micro and back. There has been considerable debate on the methodological issues of the adjustment-welfare problem, especially in the context of the Social Dimensions of Adjustment (SDA) programme of the World Bank (for a useful review see Pinstrup-Andersen, 1990). The conclusion appears to be that one needs a combination of macro-sectoral analysis as well as micro survey work.

In our own preliminary methodological investigation we shared the same opinion. However, it became clear from the beginning that examining the issue would essentially involve examining almost everything in the economy. The reason is that household welfare is influenced by the signals they receive, such as market prices, availability of services, opportunities for work, etc. These variables are all affected by macro policies, and hence a macro framework is needed to examine their changes in the face of SSAPs. However, the extent to which they affect individual households cannot be ascertained without micro information showing how individual types of households are dependent on each group of variables. Hence the issue was how to break the problem down to manageable components.

We decided at the outset to follow a multifaceted and gradualist, as well as pragmatic approach. First, we thoroughly examined all the available information and past research in order to see whether they could tell us anything about the problem. This investigation had the objective of examining past history and seeing whether the available facts were in accordance with the conventional wisdom. This was done in order to ascertain the potential pay-off from new data-collection efforts. Once this was done and the need for more information, especially of the micro type, was ascertained, two surveys were conducted, one of small-scale enterprises, and another of households at the national level. Finally, in order to further check the conclusions of the various preliminary analyses and surveys, a computable general equilibrium model (CGE) of Tanzania was constructed.

Reinterpreting Tanzanian Economic History

While there had been considerable amount of past research and analysis in Tanzania using available macro data, it soon became clear in the course of our background investigation that the picture presented by the available data was only part of the story and behind the scenes there was a whole other picture that was not captured by the existing information. Delving into this issue of reinterpreting the macro data, or checking it against other micro or sectoral information, resulted in a book (Sarris and van den Brink, 1993), in which the basic aim was to reinterpret past (mid-1970s to mid-to-late-1980s) Tanzanian developments in light of all available information.

The basic new element that we introduced and through which we tried to reinterpret the economic developments, was the size and evolution of the "second", or "underground", or "parallel", or "unofficial" economy (there are other names as well). We used a variety of techniques to ascertain the size of that economy, which presents considerable difficulties in its analysis because it is not measured. Generally our estimates were that it amounted to about 30-70 per cent of the official GDP. This is a sizeable amount and hence could potentially cloud the observed behaviour of the economy.

That this is a real possibility can be ascertained with the help of Figure 4.1, which presents a graph of the real official and estimated total (namely including the estimated unofficial and not measured) economy, according to one of the methods employed.

It can be seen that not only the total real GDP is about 30-40 per cent higher than the officially reported GDP, but more importantly, that many turning points are different. For instance the graph of estimated total GDP indicates a fall in real total GDP in 1973 (year of the Ujamaa resettlement campaign and drought) while the official series does not. Similarly the graph for total GDP indicates falls in 1979 (Uganda war) and large falls in 1982-83 (the years of the biggest crisis), while the official series indicate a rise in 1979 and a very small decline in 1982-83.

Another indication of the unreliability of official statistics can be gleamed from Table 4.1, which indicates the official (namely, used for GDP estimates) figures for production of major cereals and cassava, and estimates based on independent national sample surveys with reliable crop-cutting techniques used to estimated yields. Again

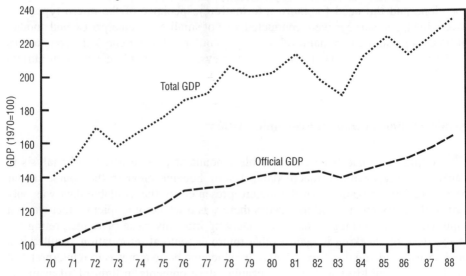

Figure 1. **Real official and total GDP in Tanzania, 1970-88**

Source: Sarris and van den Brink (1993).

Table 4.1. **Accuracy of food crop statistics**
Tanzania: comparison between official and survey-based estimates
of food production of major food staples, 1987/88
(thousand metric tons)

	Official (1)	Sample survey-based (2)	Percent difference (1) and (2)
Maize	2 339	1 799	30.0
Paddy	615	445	38.2
Sorghum	420	281	49.5
Millet	280	228	22.8
Cassava	1 709	292	485.3

Source: Sarris and van den Brick (1993).

it can be seen that the discrepancies are very large. Upon further examination, it turned out that the large discrepancies were due to the particular method of measuring agricultural production officially. The method relied on reports of regional agricultural development officers (RADOs). RADOs, however, were influenced by local officials who got credits for having a high agricultural harvest in their region. In fact it was revealed that the discrepancies started appearing at around the period when the reward system of local officials was instituted.

Our further perusal of the methods of construction of national account statistics reinforced the impression based on estimates of the underground economy, namely that the official statistics were presenting a picture different than the actual one. The grim realisation, therefore, from this first analysis was that official macro statistics could not be relied upon for any analysis of trends in incomes or welfare.

The second major realisation from the examination of the past behaviour of the Tanzanian economy, and consistent with our analysis of the macro data, was that contrary to the official claim that the economy was perfectly controlled before the onset of SSAPs (all major food and non-food markets were operating under government of parastatal control throughout the 1970s and the 1980s), in fact there was a lot of parallel activity. This was exhibited in both the parallel foreign-exchange markets, as well as in the domestic-goods markets.

Figure 4.2 shows the parallel exchange-rate premium defined as the percentage difference between the parallel and the official exchange rate from 1970 to 1989. It is clear that except for few years, the foreign-exchange market was considerably unbalanced with premia in excess of 100 per cent. Interviews with various parties also revealed that there were large amounts of illegal parallel trading with neighbouring countries all throughout the 1970s and 1980s.

Figure 2. **Tanzania — parallel exchange, rate premium**

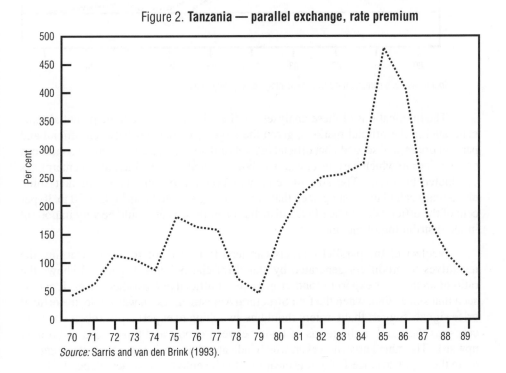

Source: Sarris and van den Brink (1993).

The existence of parallel markets, however, was not restricted to the foreign-exchange market. Figure 4.3 shows percentage differences between parallel and official market prices of major staple foods in Tanzania from 1980 to 1989 (food accounted in 1976 for about 75 per cent of rural total consumption and 65 per cent of urban total consumption). It can be seen that in the crisis period 1982-84, the parallel prices were 50-250 per cent above official prices.

Figure 3. **Tanzania — price differences open to official consumer market**

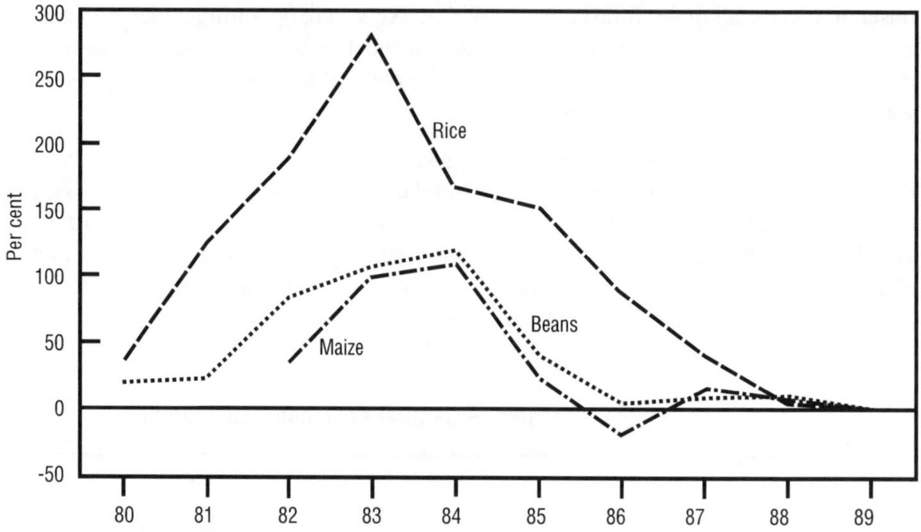

Source: Author's computations from Marketing Development Bureau data.

The implications of these analyses are first, that there were large potential rents generated in the official markets, given the large discrepancies between official and parallel prices, and second, that official markets did not represent the scarcity conditions or the prices in which various consumers bought goods, or in which many enterprises conducted business. The size of rents was potentially very large. In fact some elementary calculations suggested that potential rents could be as high as 20 to 30 per cent of the official GDP. Clearly the distribution of these rents could be very important in the distribution of income.

Neglect of the parallel markets can lead to biased inferences concerning the incentives to producers generated by stated official policies. Figure 4.4 shows the ratio of an index of export to food-crop prices at official and parallel prices. It can be seen that since 1984, when the first Structural Adjustment Loan was made, the official price signals suggest that farmers should be switching to export crops relative to food crops, as the trend in the terms of trade between export and food crops is strongly upwards. The other curve, however, which indicates the signals at parallel rates suggests quite the opposite since 1986. It is clear that the incentives to farmers depend a lot on

104

in which market the farmers were operating. Figure 4.5, which displays real official producer coffee prices and border coffee prices at official and parallel exchange rates, suggests a similar story. While real official coffee prices appear to be steadily increasing since 1984, international border prices at official exchange rates show an increase until 1988 and a fall thereafter, and international border prices at parallel exchange rates (the prices appropriate for reputedly widespread coffee smuggling) appear to have been continuously dropping since 1985.

Figure 4. **Tanzania — domestic terms of trade, export to food crops**

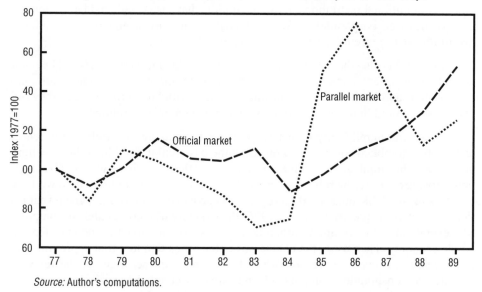

Source: Author's computations.

Figure 5. **Real coffee prices in Tanzania, 1977-91**

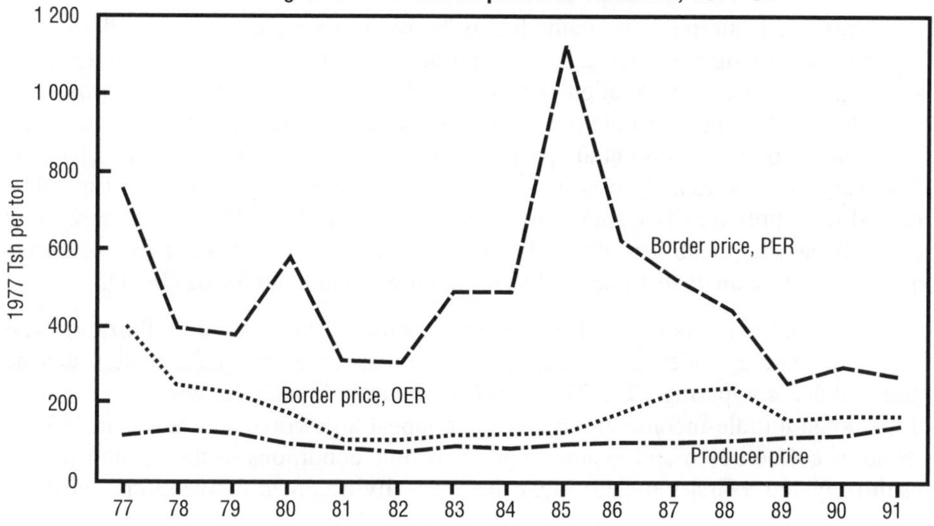

The lessons to be drawn from the above experiences are the following:

Lesson 1. In research in sSA countries one must carefully examine the construction of official statistics before drawing any conclusions about any trends.

Lesson 2. Direct controls are very difficult to enforce in sSA. Parallel markets develop that can thwart the effects of controls. Under such a system the notion of prices must be very carefully analysed.

Lesson 3. Despite attempts by many governments in sSA to modernise and eliminate traditional institutions, these institutions have survived, and have been the basis of the extensive parallel markets. In fact, it is thanks to the underlying traditional institutions that households survived throughout the periods of sSA crises.

Lesson 3 is also the conclusion of a paper by Sahn and Sarris (1994). The point is that governments, instead of attempting to eliminate traditional exchange relationships and institutions and substituting them with "modern ones", as they did in the past, should build on traditional social and economic institutions.

Given the unreliability of macro statistics for making any welfare inference, and in order to obtain some indication about the past evolution of household welfare and to test the implications of the analysis indicating that there was a substantial unobserved economy, the following methodology was devised for household welfare. By utilising available household surveys, it was possible to derive for a given year (in this case it was the pre-crisis year of 1976) the structure of incomes and consumption for several classes of rural and urban households, which altogether represented the whole economy. Then using the comparative static idea that to a first approximation small changes in welfare are proportional to changes in the prices of the relevant income and consumption components, and using observed changes in prices, it was possible to derive successive approximations to welfare changes for representative members of each class of households.

This is an intermediate methodology between a simple macro-based analysis and one based on more elaborate models or one based on micro surveys, but it has the advantage that it can be applied with relatively *easily available information.* The methodology does not attribute the changes in observed prices to any one cause, and hence cannot be used to point at specific policies as the culprit for welfare changes. However, it can be reliably used to analyse the evolution of welfare over time. The method was applied to Tanzania (Sarris and van den Brink, 1993), and because of its relatively easy applicability, also to Ghana (Sarris, 1993), and a set of sSA countries in a comparative analysis of several sSA countries (Sahn and Sarris, 1991).

Table 4.2 exhibits results from the application of the method to Tanzania. The figures indicate an index of per capita welfare over time. From the table it can be observed that comparing 1975-77 to 1987-89, household welfare, with the exception of the urban middle-income group, does not appear any worse than it was in 1976, a period of coffee boom and generally good-income conditions in the economy. This result provided a first indication that the generally accepted conventional wisdom, according to which household incomes and welfare had deteriorated substantially over time in the course of the crisis, should be reexamined. The analysis, however, until this point provided only clues and hypotheses rather than firm conclusions.

Table 4.2. **Tanzania: evolution of househols welfare, 1975-89**

| Period | Household group | | | | | |
| | Rural | | | Urban | | |
	Poor	Middle	Rich	Poor	Middle	Rich
1975-77	100.0	100.0	100.0	100.0	100.0	100.0
1978-80	100.0	98.2	93.5	98.8	88.1	99.9
1981-83	104.0	107.5	106.5	101.5	79.1	113.9
1984-86	108.4	111.1	108.5	105.5	89.2	113.3
1987-89	101.5	98.9	98.1	100.5	80.4	99.6

Source: Sarris and van den Brink (1993), Table 66.

Testing the Income-Decline Hypothesis with Micro Data

It must have become clear from the above exposition that the issues at hand could not have been resolved without the help of additional micro-level household information. Hence the next step was to design appropriate surveys. Two surveys were conducted in this context. The first one was a household-level survey, using a statistically representative national sample of a little over 1 000 households. The second one was of 540 small-scale urban enterprises (defined as those with fewer than 10 employees) using a random but not-nationally representative sample from five major cities.

The urban enterprise survey was designed in such a way as to provide information about the structure as well as the evolution of the sector that by all estimates provided the major unobserved part of the Tanzanian economy throughout the crisis period. Questions concerning present and past business conditions as well performance were asked. The analysis of the data revealed several surprises.

First it turned out that although the bulk of enterprises (40 per cent), especially the smaller ones, had been established in the period after the start of SSAP policies (namely since 1986), a significant number of the surveyed enterprises (23 per cent) had been established before 1983. In fact 11 per cent of the enterprises had been established in the peak period of the crisis (1980-83). This suggested that there was considerable unreported informal activity throughout all the period of the macroeconomic crisis.

The data on the profitability of these small enterprises (computed through a tedious process of valuation) revealed a very interesting pattern. Table 4.3 indicates the gross operating surplus of the enterprises net of owner's imputed wage cost as a ratio to the estimated current asset value of the enterprises in the survey year 1991. It can clearly be seen that the average rate of return to small-scale enterprises in 1991 was very high, averaging 120 per cent. Even accounting for large errors in the computation of asset values, the returns are quite substantial. These profitability calculations suggest first that there is a lot of potential in the small-scale enterprise sector, since high profitability means a high desire to expand (68 per cent of the enterprises were operating under conditions of excess demand for their products and with capacity constraints in 1991), and second, that consistently with the earlier observations there was a lot of parallel activity in the unobserved sector all throughout the crisis period, a factor that could have considerably biased any of the conclusions based on analysis of official data. At least the survey results did not contradict our analysis based on available official data.

Turning to the household survey, it turned out to be the first national-level household survey done in Tanzania since 1976. We found out in the process that there were a lot of practical problems in conducting it, arising both from infrastructure as well as institutional factors, but it eventually turned out that the cost was relatively low.

Table 4.3. **Tanzania: small scale urban enterprises gross operating surplus (net of owner's imputed labour cost)**

(as percentage of estimated current-asset value, 1991)

Sector of enterprise	Current assets (000 Tsh)	Return on current assets (%)
Forestry	514.4	538.8
Food manufacturing	546.8	119.6
Other consumer-goods manufacturing	64.8	541.5
Intermediate and capital manufacturing	523.7	208.1
Household industries	673.6	105.8
Construction	2 860.8	100.6
Commerce	196.5	130.0
Transport, communications	1 322.4	37.0
Health, education	730.6	20.1
Other services	826.2	35.6
Size of enterprise		
Owner only	144.4	310.6
1-2 worker(s)	566.5	85.3
3-5 workers	1 541.5	103.8
6-9 workers	1 390.9	359.2
Owner's sex		
Male	730.7	113.5
Female	208.2	71.4
All enterprises	611.6	120.1

Source: Bagachwa, Sarris et Tinios (1993).

By comparing the survey-based estimates of total national consumption with the figure suggested by the official national accounts of Tanzania, it turned out that the survey-based estimate was about 70 per cent above the official figure. This corroborated the estimates based on other methods (outlined in Sarris and van den Brink, 1993), which suggested that the unobserved economy amounted to between 40 and 70 per cent of official GDP. To further gain confidence in the survey results, a comparison was made between independent reliable survey-based estimates of production of several major (and largely non-traded) food crops, and estimated total amounts consumed nationally derived from the survey. The differences turned out to be small (in the range of 10-20 per cent) considering the differences in methodologies, definitions, etc. (see Tinios *et al.*, 1994), and this enhanced our confidence in the survey methodology and results.

Using the household survey, we attempted a comparison of real household consumption between 1976 using the earlier 1976 national household survey and the one conducted for the project (Sarris and Tinios, 1994). This, to my knowledge is the first comparison of household real incomes in sSA using surveys at two different points in time, one before the crisis and one after adjustment. Table 4.4 gives the overall results of the comparisons. It is clear that real per capita average consumption expenditures in 1991 were much higher (by 60.7 per cent) than in 1976 (a boom year). This holds both for rural and urban areas, despite the fact that the number of urban households increased considerably more than that of rural households.

The above empirical proposition was subjected to considerable sensitivity analysis by using alternative price deflators, and was found quite robust. In fact it turned out that not only average per capita consumption expenditures were higher in 1991, but also that the whole distribution of consumption expenditures improved. The income distributions of rural and urban populations in 1991 turned out to exhibit

Table 4.4. **Tanzania: comparison of real consumption expenditures in 1976/77 and 1991**

(Tsh in 1991 prices)

	1976/77	1991	Percent change between 1991 and 1976/77
Rural per household			
Total expenditure	123 908	184 760	49.1
Rural per capita			
Total expenditure	21 506	29 013	34.9
Urban per household			
Total expenditure	214 503	378 499	76.5
Urban per capita			
Total expenditure	32 984	74 203	125.0
Tanzania per household			
Total expenditure	144 870	225 382	55.6
Tanzania per capita			
Total expenditure	23 023	36 988	60.7

Source: Sarris and Tinios (1994).

considerably *lower* inequality compared with 1976. This then can be regarded as a major challenge to the conventional wisdom, which suggested that though things had improved since 1986, real household incomes as well as the distribution of income were surely much worse in 1991 than in pre-crisis years, such as 1976.

The major lesson to be learned from this experience is that in analysing household-related issues in sSA, one needs micro-survey information.

A Macro-Micro Simulation Analysis of Adjustment Impacts

The various types of analysis indicated above, while showing with reasonable confidence that welfare of most types of households in Tanzania had improved considerably after the onset of SSAPs, and also in comparison to a presumably more prosperous period, still did not attribute the improvement to any policies. Therefore, the final aspect of the project involved the construction of a counterfactual computable general equilibrium (CGE) type of model in order to separate SSAP-type policies from exogenous influences.

The model constructed was based on a social accounting matrix (SAM), which was also constructed for Tanzania (Sarris, 1994a). This SAM was based on a 1976 data set, as at the time of the analysis there was very little information available to do it for a later year.

Why does one need a CGE type of framework? The answer is that it is the only methodology currently available with which one can do counterfactual analysis, namely analyse the picture of an economy over a past period under alternative assumptions. Given this assessment, there is a host of issues related to CGE construction and operation that cannot be ignored.

The first issue concerns SAM construction. Is a SAM a good enough representation of the economy? The answer is that it is the best available description, as it incorporates all relevant and available macro and micro information. From an adjustment perspective, the most crucial element in the description of an economy is the institutional detail. For instance in the Tanzanian SAM, the incomes and expenditures of six types of households, two types of enterprises (private and parastatal), the government, and the rest of the world are separately indicated.

The second issue concerns the detail, and thus the size, of the inter-industry matrix. The lesson on that item is that the sectoral detail of the economy does not have to be too large. Detailed inter-industry classification does not matter much for adjustment types of experiment. Much more important and interesting (and also data-intensive) is the institutional detail.

The final issue concerns the specification of the model structure. It is this that makes the difference in model outcomes and not the size or detail of different sectors. Of course this is well known, and has been the subject of considerable debate within the development-economics profession (see for instance the papers in the special issue of the *Journal of Development Economics* on Income Distribution in Planning Models [Vol. 6. No. 1, March 1979]).

The most important aspect of the specification of a model is the assumed behaviour of the labour market. There exists very little analysis of labour-market conditions in Africa. In fact, while there are a lot of published series on market prices, very little, or no information, on market wages for different types of work and labour is available. However, it is the assumptions about the labour market, such as the assumption about full employment or wage rigidities that condition model outcomes.

The second most important aspect in the specification of a macrosectoral model is the behaviour of savings and investment. Despite considerable experience in model building in both developed and developing countries we know very little about the savings-cum-asset acquisition behaviour of households and the investment behaviour of firms. However, since household savings provide the bulk of investable resources in any economy while private investment constitutes the bulk of capital formation, these are areas where considerably more knowledge is necessary.

As far as dynamic behaviour is concerned, apart from the savings-investment relations the labour supply, which is tied to the labour-leisure choices of households, one needs to model the changing-skill mix of the labour force through education and on-the-job training, and the interaction of public infrastructure with capacity utilisation and production. All these factors have been found to be important for growth, especially in the 1990s debate of the "new growth theory", but very little is known about the microeconomics of how they are generated.

The model built for Tanzania is a complete macro-micro model in the sense that it incorporates a comprehensive monetary accounting, portfolio behaviour of all institutions, separate savings-investment behaviour by all institutions, parallel markets for foreign exchange and goods, wealth effects, rent creation, and asset redistribution among households due to wealth changes. It has many features similar to the maquette models designed at the OECD (Bourguignon, Branson and de Melo, 1989), but extends the specifications of that model in several directions (for an exposition, see Sarris, 1994b).

A major shortcoming of this and all other similar CGEs is that they cannot be easily calibrated over time. In other words, while the calibration to a base year is perfect, when exogenous variables are used to project a reference scenario the outcomes are not always close to some of the observed endogenous outcomes (examples are money variables, which are normally observable). A major methodological effort is needed to devise appropriate dynamic calibration techniques, in order to improve our confidence in the reference scenarios implied by the models.

In the Tanzanian model, for instance, while the behaviour over the first 4-6 years of the simulation is reasonably close to observed data (such as the consumer-price index, the money supply, parallel exchange rates, etc.) it starts to diverge after that.

This is of course understandable in view of the substantial economic repression of the economy during this period (Bevan *et al.*, 1990), which created all sorts of parallel channels of activities, only part of which can be captured by a model. This, however, does not affect the model's capability for doing comparative static exercises. In other words, although the model is not appropriate for prediction or tracking history, it is very suitable for counterfactual policy analysis.

Table 4.5 shows the results from model simulations of a SSAP composed of: 1) a devaluation of the official exchange rate by 20 per cent in all years; 2) an increase in nominal investment expenditures by 20 per cent in all years financed by a corresponding reduction in all public current expenditures; 3) a reduction by 10 per cent in all years of public-sector employment; and 4) a reduction by 20 per cent in the indirect tax rate on agricultural exports.

Table 4.5. **Simulated impact of structural adjustment programme on welfare of Tanzanian households and general economic magnitudes using a CGE model**
(all figures are percentage deviations from the reference scenario)

Household welfare by household type	Year 1	Year 2
Rural		
Poor	-0.8	1.8
Middle-income	-0.9	0.4
Rich	-4.0	0.2
Urban		
Poor	-1.2	0.4
Middle-income	-4.6	-0.9
Rich	-4.9	0.0
Real GDP per capita	0.1	3.2
Government deficit	-140.8	-47.5
Foreign official deficit	-71.0	-25.6

Source: Sarris (1994b).

The results illustrated in the table confirm the analyses based on completely different methods. In other words, the impact of adjustment programmes is rather negative in the short run (given that imports decline because of declines in net foreign capital inflows), but quite positive in the medium run. In addition, note that the only negative impact in the medium run is that on the middle-income urban households, which is what was inferred by a completely different technique in Sarris and van den Brink (1993) (Table 4.2).

The results of the model thus appear to be compatible with the survey results, as well as the analysis based on existing data. Hence one is much more confident that the results concerning the evolution of household welfare are robust.

The major overall lesson that can be drawn from the exposition of the above experience, is that given the difficulty of observation in African economies, the examination of any substantive policy issue needs a multipronged approach. In particular it appears that a combination of macro-based as well as micro-based analyses offers the best combination of policy-analysis methodologies for the current state of development in Africa.

Concluding Remarks and Areas for Future Research

The research experience described above suggests several areas of research with high pay-off in terms of knowledge useful for policy making.

(i) *Rent generation and redistribution.* It was seen above that rents are important from a macroeconomic perspective. They are also very important from an income distribution perspective. Though it is well known that rent seeking is a major aspect of the political economy of many developing countries, not enough is known about the types of institutions and policies that are conducive to generating rents.

(ii) *Household dynamics.* Household decisions are the key element of the determinants of aggregate savings but also investments, labour supply and education. Advances in household analysis in the early 1990s have emphasised the role of *consumption smoothing* as a key element of household behaviour under uncertainty in a context of imperfect credit and insurance markets. This is an area where much fruitful research remains to be done, especially in the study of *intertemporal* household decisions.

(iii) *Functioning of labour markets.* It is rather surprising that so little is known about labour markets in Africa, given the importance of them in macro adjustment. The experience in Tanzania suggests that a most fruitful area of future work concerns the micro-economic aspects of labour markets.

(iv) *Determinants of enterprise investments.* This is the subject that is crucial to understanding growth dynamics in Africa. Past policies in sSA tried to have a direct influence on private-sector investment behaviour with various policies. In the new context of more liberalised markets, private enterprises will be influenced by a different set of considerations, such as credit, infrastructure and policy, as well as political stability. Understanding of the relative importance of these factors is a priority research area.

(v) *The role of the small-scale enterprise sector.* This is the sector that has been thoroughly neglected in sSA, where policy makers were generally concerned with large-scale "modern" types of firms, neglecting the fact that small-scale enterprises, apart from being very flexible, can provide both significant employment and growth. Although the importance of this sector is starting to be

realised, it is not clear whether it constitutes a coping mechanism by households that cannot otherwise survive, or a viable alternative to the hitherto followed pattern of growth in sSA.

(vi) *Socio-economic analysis of institutional development.* In sSA, the transition from traditional to Western-style "modern" institutions was forced, and perhaps this might be one of the reasons for their widespread failure. Recent advances in the theory of endogenous institutional development suggest that changes in the underlying economic variables that create conditions are what is appropriate for the establishment of alternative institutions. In sSA there is ample room for researching both the past evolution of institutions in specific areas (for instance credit, marketing and insurance), and relate it to the underlying socioeconomic conditions.

(vii) *The microeconomics of technical change.* It is well recognised that technical change provides a key mechanism for growth and change. The experience of Southeast Asia with the Green Revolution offers ample evidence. In sSA technical change has lagged considerably behind similar changes in other regions. It is not clear whether this is due to objective factors such as the inherent inadequacy of soils or the genetic weakness of the African flora, or whether it is due to institutional factors that inhibit adaptation and innovation, but are otherwise well within the capacity of African governments to influence.

In terms of methodological approaches there are two main lessons to be learned and recommendations to be made. The first is that policy analysis in sSA is fraught with difficulties because of the unreliability of existing information. Any serious research effort should apply a multitude of techniques, and utilise both macro as well as micro information to increase the reliability of conclusions.

Second, given this sobering observation, and given that research resources are always limited, it is recommended that multi-country research efforts designed to investigate substantive issues in order to influence both local government and donor policies, should concentrate on a few representative countries, rather than attempting to get a wider diversity. The historical, cultural, and institutional similarities in sSA are such that the pay-off from future research is most likely to come from *intensive* research efforts rather than *extensive* ones, i.e. wide country coverage but with limited research resources devoted to each country case study.

References

BAGACHWA, M.S.D., A.H. SARRIS and P. TINIOS (1993), "Small Scale Enterprises in Tanzania: Results from a 1991 Survey", Cornell University Food and Nutrition Policy Program, Working Paper 44, Ithaca, N.Y., June.

BEVAN, D.L., P. COLLIER and J.W. GUNNING (1988), "Incomes in the United Republic of Tanzania during the Nyerere Experiment", *in* W. van Ginnecken, ed., *Trends in Employment and Labour Incomes*, International Labour Office, Geneva.

BEVAN, D.L., P. COLLIER and J.W. GUNNING, with A. BIGSTEN and P. HORSNELL (1990), *Peasants and Governments. An Economic Analysis*, Clarendon Press, Oxford.

BOURGUIGNON, F., W.H. BRANSON and J. de MELO (1989), "Macroeconomic Adjustment and Income Distribution: A Macro-Micro Simulation Model", OECD Development Centre, Technical Paper No. 1, Paris.

CORNIA , A.P.R., R. JOLLY, and F. STEWART (1987), *Adjustment with a Human Face*, Clarendon Press, Oxford.

PINSTRUP-ANDERSEN, P., ed. (1990), *Macroeconomic Policy Reforms, Poverty, and Nutrition: Analytical Methodologies*, Monograph 3, Cornell University Food and Nutrition Policy Program, Ithaca, N.Y., February.

SAHN, D. and A.H. SARRIS (1991), "Structural Adjustment and The Welfare of Rural Smallholders: A Comparative Analysis from Sub-Saharan Africa", *The World Bank Economic Review*, Vol. 5, No. 2, May.

SAHN D. and A.H. SARRIS (1994), "The Evolution of States, Markets, and Civil Institutions in Rural Africa", *The Journal of Modern African Studies*, Vol. 32, No. 2, June.

SARRIS, A.H. (1993), "Household Welfare during Crisis and Adjustment in Ghana", *Journal of African Economies*, Vol. 2, No. 2, October.

SARRIS, A.H. (1994a), "A Social Accounting Matrix for Tanzania", Working Paper 62, Cornell University Food and Nutrition Policy Program, Ithaca, N.Y., August.

SARRIS, A.H. (1994b), "Macroeconomic Policies and Household Welfare: A Dynamic Computable General Equilibrium Analysis for Tanzania" mimeographed, forthcoming Working Paper, Cornell University Food and Nutrition Policy Program, Ithaca, New York.

SARRIS, A. and R. van den BRINK (1993), *Household Welfare during Crisis and Adjustment in Tanzania*, New York University Press for Cornell University Food and Nutrition Policy Program, New York.

SARRIS, A.H. and P. TINIOS (1994), "Consumption and Poverty in Tanzania in 1976 and 1991: A Comparison using Survey Data", Working Paper 59, Cornell University Food and Nutrition Policy Program, Ithaca, N.Y., July.

TINIOS, P., A.H. SARRIS, H.K.R. AMANI, W. MARO, and S. ZOGRAFAKIS (1994), "Households, Consumption and Poverty in Tanzania: Results from the 1991 National Cornell-ERB Survey", Working Paper 58, Cornell University Food and Nutrition Policy Program, Ithaca, N.Y.

Chapter 5

Causes of African Development Stagnation; Policy Diagnosis and Policy Recommendations for a Long-term Development Strategy

Erik Thorbecke

A comparison of the experience of successful developing countries with that of Africa can yield interesting insights and potentially useful policy recommendations. There is need for a clear understanding of the key successful elements in the development strategies of the former in recent decades in order to evaluate their potential applicability to the conditions faced by sub-Saharan Africa today. Two related questions have to be raised before embarking on this type of comparison. First, to what extent did the initial conditions of successful development performers outside of Africa, at the outset of their take-off into sustainable growth, correspond to (or diverge from) those prevailing in Africa today? Subsidiary to this question, what is the appropriate set of non-African countries that can be used as a basis of comparison? Second, what are the key elements of successful development strategies that are transferable to the present African circumstances?

Comparison of the Development Experience of Asia and Africa

Two comprehensive evaluations of the development and public-policy performance of different Third World regions appeared in 1993 and 1994. The World Bank (1993) Report on the *East Asian Miracle* highlights the success of many of the economies in East Asia in achieving rapid and equitable growth, "often in the context of activist public policies". Although focusing primarily on what it called the "High Performing Asian Economies" (HPAEs)[1], the report contrasts the performance of the latter with that of other regions, including sSA, in a number of policy areas. A second study by Lindauer and Roemer (1993) is even more germane to the topic at hand, as it directly compares the different strategies and performances of Asia and Africa since 1960.

On the basis of a thorough evaluation of different sectors, policy areas and political-economy issues, Lindauer and Roemer (1993) conclude that

> the difference in performance [between Africa and Asia] has been substantially, though not entirely, due to policy differences ... that African countries intent on changing their economic fortunes can do so, and that South-East Asia, in preference to East Asia, would be a good model for Africa.

Thus, they focus largely in their comparison on the newly industrialised economies of Indonesia, Malaysia and Thailand, in addition to the Four Tigers of East Asia, and occasionally China. We will henceforth refer to this set of countries as "Asia".

The first question Lindauer and Roemer (1993) raise is: "Why has Asia grown faster than Africa?" An obvious answer is that Asia invested significantly more than Africa. The average investment to GDP ratio in Africa between 1965 and 1990 was 17.3 per cent compared with 30.6 per cent for East and Southeast Asia (see Table 5.1). Nonetheless, even the African countries (i.e. Cameroon, Côte d'Ivoire, Kenya and Zambia) that invested around 20 per cent of their GDP — a ratio not significantly different from that of Indonesia (21.1 per cent) and Chinese Taipei (23.8 per cent) — did not even come close to approximating the latters' GDP growth rates per capita. To understand better the dynamics of the growth process, the authors undertake a simple growth accounting exercise in order to distinguish the part played by the growth of the factors of production *per se* (capital and labour force) from that of the residual growth attributable to gains in human capital and productivity. The fourth column of Table 5.1 gives rough estimates of growth rates of total factor productivity (calculated as a residual) for both sets of countries. The contrast between African countries (excepting Botswana and Cameroon) and Asia is striking. On average, total factor productivity (TFP) growth during 1965-90 was significantly positive (2.4 per cent per annum) in Asia, whereas it was negative in sSA (-0.4 per cent per annum).

The new growth economics explain TFP growth as being largely determined by investment in education and other forms of human capital, in addition to the adoption of state-of-the-art technologies, often linked to exports. On both counts, Africa lags significantly behind Asia. Although the stock of education (average years of education per adult) in Asia in 1960 (at the onset of their take-off) looked fairly similar to that of African countries in the mid-1980s, Asia has progressed enormously in the intervening years so that today a large education gap prevails between the two regions[2]. In terms of technology adoption, the World Bank (1993) estimated that sSA's ability to have kept pace with international best practices between 1960 and 1989 actually deteriorated at a rate of 3.5 per cent a year. In comparison, Asia performed much better in adopting more efficient technologies and adapting them to the local environment.

Lindauer and Roemer (1993) explain the superior performance of Asia over the last three decades under three inter-related categories: 1) patterns of governance and economic strategy; 2) use of factor endowments; and 3) components of development strategy.

Under "governance and economic strategy", the authors identify a set of key factors that helps explain the relative development success of Asia in contrast with Africa. These factors are a) political stability; b) the priority given to socioeconomic development, among other policy objectives, by the regime; c) the type of rent-seeking behaviour; d) the treatment of entrepreneurially able ethnic minorities; and, e) the insulation of economic policy-making from politics. Although political stability is neither a necessary nor a sufficient condition for development to occur; in combination with other elements it can contribute to its achievement. On the whole, Asian regimes enjoyed somewhat greater stability than Africa. The priority assigned to development in the preference function of regimes has often been related to their rent-seeking behaviour. Asian leaders understood that rapid growth was essential to the survival of their regimes (as in Indonesia and Malaysia) or even the survival of their countries (as in Korea, Chinese Taipei and Singapore)[3]. Although all Asian regimes engaged (to a greater or lesser degree) in rent-seeking behaviour, most of them understood that "growing rents require growing economies ... [and that] ... when rent-seeking threatened sound economies, the rents were curbed" — a lesson that many African leaders have yet to learn!

The contrast between the treatment of entrepreneurially able ethnic minorities in Asia and Africa is great. Lindauer and Roemer (1993) argue convincingly that ethnic Chinese have played major— if not dominant — roles in commerce and industry in Indonesia, Malaysia and Thailand despite strong popular pressure for their suppression. On the other hand, such minorities as the Lebanese in West Africa and ethnic Indians in East Africa have tended to be overtly discriminated against in much of Africa. Many sSA governments have pushed through "Africanisation" processes that starved their countries, at least in the short to medium run, of skilled entrepreneurs.

Finally, Asia has been much more successful in insulating the design and conduct of economic policy from politics, through the establishment of relatively strong and independent institutions such as planning boards, finance ministries and central banks. For example, Indonesia during the Suharto period (i.e. since 1967) has relied, at least until a year ago, on a cadre of well-trained economic technocrats (the so-called "Berkeley Mafia") in the formulation and implementation of its economic development strategy. It also instituted automatic rules such as a constitutional balanced-budget amendment reducing significantly the scope for central-bank credit creation and inflationary policies. An interesting point made by Lindauer and Roemer (1993) is that Southeast Asian countries —- suffering more from clientelism and rent-seeking than East Asia — wisely relied more on the market than did Korea and Chinese Taipei. For example, they mention that export growth in Southeast Asia came from smaller firms and from agriculture "guided by market incentives, not by government". By inference, African policy makers should select strategies that are no more interventionist than those in Southeast Asia.

Table 5.1. **Growth, resources and productivity, 1965-90**

	GDP per capita	Population	Annual growth rate (% p.a.) Exports: goods + non-factor services[1]	Total factor productivity[2]	Ratio (%) investment to GDP
East/Southeast Asia	5.3	1.9	13.5	2.4	30.6
Korea	7.3	1.7	18.9	4.9	26.7
Chinese Taipei	6.9	1.9	15.2	4.9	23.8
Hong Kong	6.1g	2.0g	11.0g	3.6g	29.7g
Singapore	7.0	1.9	12.1n	3.6	35.3
China	6.1a	2.2a	13.6	2.7	21.1
Indonesia	4.3	2.2	13.6	2.7	21.1
Malaysia	3.0	2.7	8.7	1.1	25.4
Philippines	1.4	2.7	7.2	0.0	20.7
Thailand	5.1	2.5	10.5	3.3	24.3
Sub-Saharan Africa	0.2	2.9	4.5	-0.4	17.3f
Botswana	7.9	3.7	15.9c	6.4	28.0c
Cameroon	1.5h	1.8	4.4k	2.5k	20.2k
Chad	-0.6g	2.2	1.3g	n.d.	n.d.
Côte d'Ivoire	-0.7g	3.9f	4.8m	-0.7k	20.0d
Ghana	-0.7	2.7	1.5	-0.8	9.6
Kenya	1.3c	3.8	3.3a	0.2g	20.5e
Mali	1.8g	2.3	6.3g	1.2g	13.2g
Nigeria	2.1f	2.8	10.9f	1.3f	17.4f
Senegal	-0.3g	3.2	2.5j	-0.6j	14.1
Tanzania	0.3	3.2	3.0	-0.7	19.7

Table 5.1. (cont.)

	GPD per capita	Population	Annual growth rate (% p.a.) Exports: goods + non-factor services[1]	Total factor productivity[2]	Ratio (%) investment to GDP
Zaire	-3.0f	2.0	-4.5f	-4.3f	14.6
Zambia	-1.9a	2.7	-1.3h	-3.1b	21.1b
Zimbabwe	1.0g	3.0	3.8h	-0.5f	18.1f
Developing countries	2.5	2.2	7.4	0.4	24.8f

Notes:
1.   Revenues from exports of goods, plus non-factor services in constant US dollars.
2.   Total factor productivity calculated by the approximation explained in note 3 of text. Regional averages are roughly indicative only, as they use figures in this table which are not all for the same year.

a: 1965-89; b: 1965-88; c: 1965-87; d: 1965-86; e: 1967-89; f: 1970-90; g: 1970-89; h: 1970-88; i: 1970-87; j: 1970-86; k: 1970-85; m: 1971-86; n: 1975-89

Sources: Lindauer and Roemer (1993).

With regard to factor endowment, it appears that Asia largely followed the dictates of comparative advantage. East Asian countries that were well endowed with unskilled labour based their development strategies first on agriculture— pushing through major land reforms insuring a single mode of land distribution — before gradually moving into labour-intensive manufacturing exports. Similarly, the NIEs in Asia at first relied extensively on primary-product exports before diversifying into labour-intensive manufacturing products. As the Four Tigers gradually switched from producing textiles to producing more advanced products, countries such as Indonesia, the Philippines and Thailand began to capture a larger share of the textile market.

A crucial difference between Asia and Africa lies in the treatment of, and strategy, *vis-à-vis* the agricultural sector. During the structural transformation, when the centre of gravity of the economy gradually moves away from agriculture towards non-agriculture, an agricultural surplus has to be generated and captured to help finance the industrialisation phase. The process of capturing the surplus is quite delicate. The goal should be to generate a reliable and continuous flow of *net* resources from agriculture into the rest of the economy throughout much of the structural transformation. A lesson learned from the HPAEs is that a continuing *gross* flow of resources should be provided to agriculture to increase this sector's productivity and potential capacity of contributing an even larger return flow to the rest of the economy. It is much easier to extract a net surplus from increasing production than from stagnant or falling output (Thorbecke and Morrisson, 1989).

In the successful Asian countries, the state set up a whole set of institutions (covering such areas as research, marketing, distribution of inputs and products, extension and credit) and invested heavily in physical infrastructure (e.g. irrigation schemes and farm-to-market roads). The gross flow of resources into agriculture embedded into these activities accelerated the adoption of more efficient technologies and led to a rapid output growth — particularly in paddy (rice) production. The improved transportation and distribution network also helped integrate markets and fuel competition. The high rate of technological progress in agriculture and the rising output kept agricultural prices down relatively to non-agricultural prices and made it easier for the government to siphon off a larger gross flow of taxes and revenues from that sector so as to generate a net transfer. In contrast, in many African countries, the package of institutions (e.g. marketing boards) and various other measures and forms of taxation in agriculture were so extractive that they discouraged the growth of agricultural output. For example, artificial price policies favouring consumers at the expense of producers affected farmers' incentives negatively and usually resulted in rationing and parallel markets.

The poor state of the transportation network in much of Africa has led to segmented markets and much higher marketing margins than in Asia. In a comparison of two types of price spreads in food grain markets estimated for five African and four Asian countries, respectively, Ahmed and Rustagi (1984) found that average producer prices expressed as a percentage of final consumer prices in the African countries ranged from 30 per cent to 60 per cent, whilst in Asia they ranged from

75 per cent to 90 per cent. Thus, African farmers received a significantly smaller proportion of final consumer prices of marketed food grains than did their Asian counterparts.

Another significant difference between Asia and Africa that helps explain the low supply response in agriculture in the latter relates to the behaviour of farmers facing shortages of inputs and manufactured goods (such as chemical fertilizer, soap, textile fabrics, beer and matches). It has been demonstrated that when such shortages prevail, or when these goods were only available at usurious prices (as in Ghana and Tanzania, at least until the mid-1980s), farmers tended to lose any incentive to produce for the market (Berthélemy and Morrisson, 1989; Bevan *et al.*, 1987)[4]. The result of such shortages is a reversion to a subsistence economy, which is further accelerated by the existence of a wide spread between farm gate prices and prices paid by consumers (de Janvry *et al.*, 1991). Both shortages of manufactured inputs and consumer goods, and wide bands between prices paid by consumers and prices received by farmers have been endemic in many African countries — in contrast with Asia.

A final strategic distinction between key Southeast Asian countries and their counterparts in Africa relates to how the proceeds of primary-product exports (particularly the windfall profits from booming cocoa and coffee prices in the 1970s and the oil-price windfall before 1983) were used. In Southeast Asia (particularly Indonesia and Malaysia) a large part of these proceeds was reinvested into agriculture, mainly in the form of irrigation, other physical infrastructure projects and fertilizer subsidies benefiting small rice producers. Through this mechanism, combined with well-timed devaluations to avoid a process of currency appreciation that would have hurt traditional export sectors, Indonesia and Malaysia avoided the "Dutch disease" that plagued Nigeria and some other African countries.

Differences in development strategies are the final reasons given by Lindauer and Roemer (1993) and the World Bank (1993) for the superior Asian performance. Very briefly, macro management in the seven HPAEs was characterised by sound fiscal policies resulting in low budget deficits; conservative monetary policies keeping inflation down to less than 10 per cent per annum; the maintenance of (equilibrium) exchange-rates very close to their free-market rates; and currency convertibility. The contrast with most of Africa is dramatic. In particular, the premium on the parallel market for foreign exchange in 1981-86 was estimated to be just short of 300 per cent of the official exchange rate for sub-Saharan adjusting countries with flexible exchange-rates (World Bank, 1994). Finally, there were also significant differences in the types of industrial strategies followed by these two groups of countries.

Policy Diagnosis and Recommended Components of a Long-term Development Strategy for sSA

The orthodox viewpoint is that stabilisation and structural adjustment programmes (SSAPs) represent the appropriate policy response to the African economic crisis of the 1980s, which was itself largely the result of poor economic policies followed in the 1960s and 1970s. After more than a decade of implementation of SSAPs in sSA and based on evidence from 29 adjusting countries, the World Bank (1994) concluded that reforms pay off, and that countries that went further than others in the implementation of reforms experienced a turnaround in their growth rates and overall socioeconomic conditions — though not yet at a sustainable level. The poor performance (or development failure) observed in the 1980s is largely ascribed to the inappropriate implementation of "sound" policies, as articulated in the SSAPs. The factors that seem to have prevented the proper implementation of adjustment policies are numerous. A number of World Bank studies have noted constraints such as the difficulties in implementing politically sensitive institutional reforms (in the light of powerful vested interests), the lack of ownership of the programme by the government, inadequate external financing or under-funded programmes, the weak existing administrative and institutional capabilities in sSA to implement reforms, and on occasion unrealistic speed and sequencing of reforms imposed in various programmes (for instance, see Thomas *et al.* 1991.)

Given the experience acquired in programme implementation in Africa over more than a decade, the World Bank (1994) recommends a continuation of structural adjustment in areas "where there is consensus" and "rethinking" the design of adjustment in areas "where there is less consensus" along three guiding principles, namely "getting macroeconomic policies right, encouraging competition, and using scarce institutional capacity wisely".

According to proponents of the heterodox approach, the main cause of development failure in sSA resides in the failure of *1)* the post-independence economic policies of the 1960s and 1970s, and *2)* the SSAPs of the 1980s to address the structural weaknesses in sSA economies and institutions effectively. They characterise these weaknesses primarily as a distorted trade structure with an over-dependence on primary commodities, a lack of modernisation in agriculture, a limited and weak industrial base, and chiefly an extremely low level of human-resource development and an inadequate transport and rural infrastructure (Cornia, 1991). In the discussion of the heterodox design of a long-term development strategy for sSA, it will become evident that seeking solutions to the latter weakness is critical. While the heterodox writers do not seem to put the entire blame for economic stagnation in sSA on adjustment programmes *per se*, they do stress, however, that the almost exclusive emphasis of these programmes on short-term stabilisation measures, rather than the above deep-rooted structural impediments, is in fact moving African economies away from a long-term sustainable growth path (Cornia, 1991; Stewart, 1992). As Mosley and Toye (1987) put it:

Given the fundamental objective of trying to make markets 'work better' the Bank has arbitrarily chosen, in this phase of experiment, to attack only those structural bottlenecks, or market distortions, that are policy-induced and to ignore those which are endemic to the prevailing structure of law and society, for example failure of the market for rural credit or the absence of incentive to small tenant farmers to produce for the market.

The heterodox approach further argues that these structural weaknesses might even impinge on the achievement of short-run macro stability that seems to have been the major focus of orthodox SSAPs (Cornia, van der Hoeven, and Mkandawire, 1992). It should also be noted that the weak existing administrative and institutional capabilities that have hindered the proper implementation of SSAPs are, themselves, related to the low level of human capital prevailing today in much of Africa. It is revealing and symptomatic, in this regard, that the World Bank (1994) employs the term "using scarce institutional capacity wisely" rather than some alternative formulation such as "expanding the existing institutional capacity" as a guiding principle in future implementations of SSAPs.

Agricultural and Rural Strategy

Both the orthodox and heterodox approaches agree that past policy regimes discriminated against agriculture through implicit and explicit taxation, and that current policies should move towards reducing or eliminating the anti-rural bias and allocating more resources to agriculture. However, the heterodox approach argues that price reform *rightfully* included in orthodox reforms is incomplete, and that special attention should therefore be paid to building the needed complementary infrastructure and institutions in order to increase supply responsiveness and sustain a rising level of production in agriculture. In addition to market-determined and more stable prices, largely included in current orthodox reforms, they propose an agrarian reform package based on land reform, increased investment and human capital formation, and an extended access to inputs (Stewart, 1992; Cornia, van der Hoeven, and Mkandawire, 1992).

Of these proposed additional reforms, land reform is clearly a major undertaking and a sensitive issue. Measures are supposed to vary depending on whether land in a given country is abundant, or moderately or highly constrained. In the former case, improvement in land-tenure systems through better land conservation strategies should be emphasised, while in the latter case emphasis should be put on redistributing land surpluses from the plantation, parastatal and large farm sectors to the landless and land-deficient farmers. In cases where land is only moderately constrained, the reform can include measures such as land ceilings or the taxation of land beyond a given ceiling. The objective is to avoid future land concentration. In addition, a system of property rights is suggested in order to allow the use of land as collateral by farmers.

There exists a great variability of social, legal and cultural land-tenure settings across different countries and even regions of Africa so that no simple and general land reform model applies uniformly. There are, however, a few reasonably robust recommendations that can be made. The case for unambiguous property rights is convincing. The issuance of land titles confers many advantages to owners, i.e. *1)* greater security with land rights over time (which might encourage private investment on one's land); *2)* reduction in uncertainty regarding the outcome of adjudication of land ownership disputes; and *3)* availability of a legally recognised collateral (a *sine qua non* of access to the formal rural credit market for small farmers). The example of East Asia and many countries in South-East Asia is that private ownership of land provides a strong incentive to invest in land improvement and maximise land productivity over time. The reasons for the slow progress in developing a cadastral and land-title system vary from one setting to another, but appear to be generally related to political opposition from groups (including the state) that stand to lose from a land reform; and the enormous complexity and expensive nature of such a process. Even though it is normally taken for granted that, on efficiency grounds, official registration of land titles to individuals should be favoured, in certain settings group titling might, in fact, be consistent with improving agricultural performance. Platteau (1990) gives a number of reasons for providing group titling such as saving on budgetary expenditures and transaction costs; increasing flexibility in patterns of land use, and various potential economies of joint farming. The granting and recognition of communal rights bears directly on the metaphor of the "tragedy of the commons". In an interesting study of organisations and their impact on "sustainable development" in Africa, Vivian (1991) presents concrete examples of communal groups that appear to have been successful in efficient and sustainable resource management.

The case for complementary investment in agricultural research and physical infrastructure is compelling. Getting prices right is — at best — only one blade of a pair of scissors. There is strong evidence that the growth of total factor productivity in sSA is highly correlated with public expenditures on agricultural research (Block, 1994) and that the latter tended to be curtailed during the adjustment process. Likewise, an inadequate transportation and distribution network can raise the marketing and other transaction costs so much that, even in the presence of attractive prices, farmers' incentives to increase output vanish and they revert largely to producing for their own subsistence. We endorse the conclusions reached by Jaeger (1992) on the basis of a comprehensive analysis of economic policies in African agriculture.

> In specific countries, prices may appear to be less important than non-price factors; where price policies have not led to major distortions, attention should rightly be placed on promoting productive private and public investments. Where price distortions have been large and as a result agricultural investments neglected, both price and non-price constraints are likely to be binding, but removing price distortions should be seen as a prerequisite to encouraging appropriate investment in the sector.

The dilemma faced by adjusting countries is how to balance short-term cuts in public expenditures with the long-term need for improving the physical infrastructure and financing agricultural research. Given the very limited public resource base that these countries can tap, it appears that one partial solution to this dilemma lies in a change in the composition of external funding. Specifically, increasing the share of agricultural Sector Adjustment Loans (SECALs) while reducing that of generalised programme loans (SALs) in the World Bank lending portfolio suggests itself. A main advantage is that transfers imbedded in agricultural SECALs contribute directly to the building of physical infrastructure projects and the funding of an agricultural research network (i.e. a tangible productive counterpart) instead of taking the form of undifferentiated programme and balance-of-payments support. When properly designed, agricultural SECALs need not reduce the conditionality leverage as is sometimes argued. In fact, it allows conditionality requirements to be expressed in much more concrete and specific terms.

The importance of rural non-agricultural activities as a major source of rural employment (constituting 10-25 per cent of primary rural employment in Africa), in general, and of poor rural household incomes, in particular, is recognised in both the orthodox and heterodox approaches (Haggblade *et al.*, 1989; Stewart, 1992)[5]. Specifically, the proponents of the heterodox approach envision a crucial role to be played by rural non-agricultural activities in strengthening linkages between agricultural and non-agricultural activities through, for instance, greater support to rural industries. Both sides argue that these linkages are crucial to the development of a more labour-intensive and a more regionally balanced industrialisation process. Measures for the development of linkages include rural education more focused on technical areas, improving access of small-scale borrowers to credit institutions, establishing systems of technology dissemination, and chiefly the development of adequate physical and social infrastructure such as rural roads and electrification, and market development.

Industrialisation Strategy

Both the orthodox and heterodox approaches agree that the pattern of industrialisation of sSA has been highly deficient (i.e. highly protected). Evaluating past patterns of industrialisation in sSA, Stewart (1992) recommends an industrialisation strategy based on small-scale labour-intensive production, and temporary and selective protection. She argues that "despite some successes, the overall assessment of past patterns of industrialisation from the perspective of capacity utilisation, industrial linkages, growth in productivity, reduced dependence on foreign management and technology and exports, must be negative." Four types of explanation are suggested for the failure of industrialisation. The first explanation (which is the rationale for current orthodox SSAPs) is related to a poor incentive framework largely due to inward-oriented trade policies (i.e. heavy protection) and price distortions (mainly through pervasive government intervention). The second explanation (favoured by most African governments) points to external shocks causing import drought and starving industry of needed imports of intermediate and capital goods. The third explanation stresses the lack of human resources, skills and institutions that "facilitate the smooth functioning of markets and the creation of skills ..." (Lall, 1990). This explanation clearly occupies a central place in most heterodox diagnoses of development failure in sSA. Finally, the fourth explanation argues that policies have been biased against the "efficient" indigenous small-scale sector, which could have accounted for not only a sizeable share of industrial output but could have also been the basis for the creation of "efficient medium-sized firms, owned and controlled locally" (Stewart, 1992).

Furthermore, based on past African experiences with foreign direct investment (FDI), the heterodox approach is sceptical of the role of FDI for promoting privatisation, enhancing industrial efficiency and improving the capital account of the balance of payments. Stewart (1992) even claims that FDI can have a negative impact on the balance of payments. The low level of efficiency achieved by FDI (and probably the current slow response of FDI even in countries with large improvement in macro policy such as Ghana) is attributed to the structural constraints facing African industry, i.e. a distorted policy environment, a very low level of institutional capabilities, poor infrastructure and shortage of foreign exchange. Instead, a type of joint venture combined with some "nominal control [through ownership of capital]" is recommended as more likely to help develop African ownership and managerial capabilities than a simple form of "undiluted" FDI.

From the above diagnosis of the causes of industrial failure in sSA, the heterodox approach calls for a "more integrated role" for industrialisation, which will pay special attention to the informal sector or small-scale firms, rebuild rural industries, and provide a "selective" competitive environment for the development of medium to large-scale modern industries (Cornia, van der Hoeven and Mkandawire, 1992). The need to strengthen the link between the informal sector and the formal public and private sector is stressed. The role of macro and meso policies in supporting the informal sector is crucial in this regard. Some heterodox writers have even argued that there is no longer an urban bias, and that the focus of policies should be increasingly on alleviating urban poverty and the lot of urban unskilled workers (Jamal and Weeks, 1993). They further argue that distortions against the informal sector should be removed and additional support (e.g. access to credit) should be granted to the urban informal sector. Fiscal, monetary and exchange-rate policies should be designed so as to ensure that the informal sector has access to scarce resources, in particular foreign exchange. Stewart (1992) suggests a system of "structured market" that would guarantee that a share of needed scarce resources, such as credit and foreign exchange, is allocated to the small-scale sector since the latter, though dynamic, cannot compete with large established firms in a more conventional free-market setting (because of its lack of collateral, for instance). In addition, meso policies would aim at developing and strengthening institutions such as the financial sector, rural banks and savings schemes. The other subcomponent of the industrialisation strategy, namely the rebuilding of rural industries, will permit not only a better articulation of agricultural and industrial development but will also allow an efficient use of "abundant" low-skilled labour, particularly labour surpluses resulting from the seasonal slowdown in agricultural activities.

Finally, proponents of the heterodox approach strongly recommend a competitive environment largely characterised by "selective" protection contrasting with the trade liberalisation policies advocated in the orthodox approach. The argument here is that the previously highly protected (thus inefficient) sSA industries cannot compete internationally in the context of the orthodox "undifferentiated" import liberalisation. The latter may even further reinforce the deindustrialisation trend that occurred in sSA in the 1980s (Stewart, 1992). Therefore, a selective protection approach would aim at maintaining price controls for a few basic commodities, eliminating import quotas and restricting imports mainly through tariffs (also emphasised in the orthodox SSAPs), and granting both temporary and selective protection to be phased out over a 10-year period as efficiency increases. It should be selective in being granted only to genuine "infant industries" in sectors where dynamic comparative advantage is warranted over the temporary protection phase. The objective is that these infant industries mature into competitive export industries and thereby contribute in time to export diversification.

The case for removing discriminatory measures against the informal sector is compelling. For a long time to come the informal sector in Africa must continue to play the role of a labour sponge and therefore should, at the very least, not be at a competitive disadvantage. How far the government should go in providing further support to that sector is a difficult question to answer. At a minimum the improvement of the urban transportation and distribution network would help reduce marketing and other transaction costs borne by small, essentially service-oriented informal enterprises. Vocational and other forms of training adding to the human capital of the unskilled informal workers can contribute to enhancing their productivity.

On the other hand, an industrial strategy predicated on a "structured market" (i.e. reserving a share of credit and foreign exchange for small firms) and selective protection raises all kinds of questions. Does a typical African government (civil service) have the technical know-how to pick winners? What African government has the administrative ability to set up "contests" among protected firms à la Chinese Taipei and South Korea to wean them gradually into facing the discipline of the world market? In an environment characterised by rent-seeking and clientelism and where the civil service is not insulated from politics, is it likely that decisions will be made on efficiency grounds? The answers to each of these questions are more likely to be negative than positive. As the experience of the NIEs in Asia demonstrated, under fairly similar initial conditions, it may be wiser under the circumstances to rely largely on market and free-trade policies and minimise interventionist policies.

Furthermore, the premise of the heterodox school according to which industries in sSA are not competitive needs to be put to the test. A recent study carrying the title "Africa Can Compete" (Biggs *et al.*, 1994) maintains that producers of standardised garments in Africa (case studies were conducted in five countries: Côte d'Ivoire, Ghana, Kenya, Senegal and Zimbabwe) have become competitive with Asian rivals in countries where structural-adjustment programmes have improved the economic environment. The study gathered data on labour costs and task-level efficiency, and determined that African labour is competitive with Asian labour on both counts in factories run by experienced managers, and also identified a number of supply constraints and the role of the World Bank in helping to remove them.

Trade Strategy

In addition to the selective protection to be granted to infant industries deemed viable, the heterodox approach makes policy recommendations in two additional areas, 1) regional trade and regional import substitution, and 2) export diversification. Proponents of this approach argue that the small size of most sSA countries is unsuitable for efficient import substitution (i.e. one that will yield economies of scale, a greater division of labour, specialisation and competition allowing dynamic comparative advantage to take place). Consequently, a strategy of dynamic regional import substitution (i.e. with an eye towards future export possibilities) is proposed, based on regional trade agreements that remove or eliminate most impediments to regional trade[6]. Some authors have suggested that Nigeria and the Republic of South Africa could operate as growth poles for such regional agreements.

The worldwide experience with relatively small regional trade agreements (e.g. in East Africa, Central America and Latin America) has been uniformly discouraging. Practically all these agreements have ended up as dismal failures. The smaller the integrating group of countries, the greater the likelihood of trade diversion. If the whole of sSA (including Nigeria) could be integrated into one common market, it would, of course, increase the scope for trade creation. Such an arrangement might prove to be extremely difficult to implement in practice. In sum, such agreements should be approached with scepticism.

With respect to the issue of export diversification a major heterodox criticism of current SSAPs is that the latter have put too much emphasis on increasing the supply of exports of traditional primary commodities. As a consequence African countries remain overdependent for their export earnings on a few primary commodities facing unstable world prices. This strategy of continued reliance on primary exports can have at least three types of negative impacts according to the heterodox school. First, it fails to induce a desirable structural transformation that would increase the resilience of African economies to external shocks. Second, it tends to depress the food-crop sector (food supply, nutrition and calorie intakes)[7]. Third, it can potentially contribute to declining world prices and a deterioration of the terms of trade because of the limited world demand for primary commodities (Bhaduri,

1993). In some cases export earnings may actually fall as a result of an increase in the aggregate supply, especially for countries with a large share of the world export market for particular commodities (e.g. cocoa for Côte d'Ivoire). This third impact is often referred to as the "adding-up" problem. The empirical basis for the adding-up problem is usually provided by a comparison of income and price elasticity with shares of world exports for specific commodities, and the combined effect of low elasticity and high market shares can give rise to the adding-up problem (i.e. increased output resulting in reduced export earnings).

On the basis of the former two points, and given that most primary commodities tend to exhibit low elasticity, the heterodox approach emphasises the need to diversify exports away from traditional primary commodities towards non-traditional crops facing higher price and income elasticity as well as exports of manufactured goods. With respect to traditional crops with low elasticity, Stewart (1992) suggests a collective action among producers aimed at managing supply.

On the other hand, the orthodox position is that sSA should try first to recapture its past market shares of world exports in primary commodities[8]. Based on estimates of short- and long-run revenue elasticity of major commodities for sSA, the World Bank (1994) argues that the adding-up problem that most critics point at may hold for some commodities (such as cocoa and to a lesser extent coffee, sisal, tea and tobacco) but not for all commodities. Elasticity estimates from both the World Bank (1994) and another source are reported in Table 5.2 (the only negative revenue elasticity reported is for cocoa in the short run). The World Bank further argues that even in cases where the adding-up problem is evident there is still some scope for increased exports through, for instance, "appropriate productivity-enhancing technologies" that can make it possible to reduce the marginal cost of the additional production at a level below the long-run revenue elasticity of the particular commodity.

Regarding the issue of sSA venturing into labour-intensive manufactured exports, the World Bank suggests that sSA should proceed gradually and with a very limited amount of government intervention. The role of the government would primarily consist of providing a distortion-free policy environment, as well as export-support services, to exporters both in the short and long run. In the short run, the government can support exporters through "easier access to inputs, advantageous credit arrangements, and assistance in entering new markets"; while in the long run, government actions should aim at co-ordinating development efforts in the areas of "education curriculum and the location of infrastructure with the needs of exporters" (World Bank, 1994). The World Bank also views the importance of joint ventures with foreign firms as a possible option for sSA to break into world export markets.

In conclusion, it is clear that the scope for significant growth of primary products exports in sSA is limited. Over the last few decades Africa has lost a significant share of most of these products to other regions and with appropriate policies, it should be able to recapture a part of these losses. Hence, the potential scope for African export growth of these commodities is higher than the very limited projected growth of

Table 5.2. **Production levels and revenue elasticity, and demand elasticity**
for selected commodities, sub-Saharan Africa

| Commodity | World Bank estimates (1989/90)[1] | | | | Islam and Subramanian estimates[2] | |
| | Average production | | Revenue elasticity | | | |
	Thousands of tons	% world production	Short-term	Long-term	Income elasticity	Price elasticity
Cocoa	1 322	54.5	-0.19	0.33	0.18	-
Sisal	110	29.2	0.43	0.80	-	-0.18
Coffee	1 258	20.7	0.64	0.80	0.47	-0.27
Tea	299	16.3	0.68	0.83	0.52	0.06
Pineapples	1 242	12.3	0.84	0.92	1.59	-2.67
Tobacco						
Burley	82	10.3	0.79	0.87	-	-
All	335	4.6	0.91	0.95	-	-
Vegetable oil	3 030	5.5	0.92	0.96	-	-
Cotton	957	5.4	0.88	0.95	-	-
Sugar	3 918	3.7	0.94	0.97	-	-
Oranges	725	1.2	0.98	0.99	-	-
Bananas & plantains	-	-	-	-	0.58	-0.40
Tomatoes	-	-	-	-	1.63	0.17

[1]   Estimated by Akiyama and Larson (1993) and taken from World Bank (1994).
[2]   Taken from Stewart (1992).
-        not available.

world demand. It is also very questionable that smallholders producing export crops are at a nutritional disadvantage *vis-à-vis* food-crop producers. The solution in the long run must lie in expanding manufactured exports. Here again, lessons can be learned from the gradual transition in export composition that occurred in East and Southeast Asia. An outward-orientation centred on manufactured exports generates major positive externalities. Entrepreneurs and engineers become acquainted with, and adopt new technologies. In turn, technicians and workers operating those technologies learn by doing and by observing. Those effects contribute significantly to their human capital. Other positive inter-industry and inter-sectoral spill-over effects have been observed as entrepreneurs, engineers and workers move from one firm (sector) to another.

Investment in Human Capital

Both the orthodox and heterodox approaches stress the role of human capital as a critical component of a successful development strategy. The lessons of Asia in this regard are convincing. There appear, however, to exist some differences over *1)* the relative emphasis that should be placed on human-capital formation within the various components and policies of a long-term development strategy, and *2)* the best method to promote education. Heterodox authors seem to assign a somewhat more crucial role to human-capital formation and call for increased government expenditures (largely through budget reallocation) towards greater current and capital expenditures on education. Mosley (1990) further suggests a thorough restructuring of aid flows to sSA so that larger relative and absolute transfers are directed towards the education sector. This last point has merits. Here again, as in the case for physical infrastructure investment — and in the light of the severe budgetary constraints faced by African governments — a strong case can be made for educational SECALs. The advantage of this method of transfer is that it is earmarked for a specific set of projects and other activities in education, and that the external funds are directly channelled into a real output counterpart (e.g. the building of schools, the provision of educational supplies and the training of teachers).

Another point of divergence between the two approaches lies in the financing of education. Cornia, van der Hoeven and Mkandawire (1992) argue that orthodox adjustment policies have put too much emphasis on short-term, market-oriented measures, such as cost recovery and a greater role for the private sector, in an area where the greatest need is for government intervention as a result of the significant divergence between the private and social rates of return[9].

Speed and Sequencing of Policy Reforms

There is no firm consensus in the literature on the broad issue of the appropriate speed and sequencing of policy reforms in both adjusting economies and countries undergoing the transition from central planning to reliance on market forces. Authors such as Edwards and Krueger favour a rapid ("cold turkey") process while others (e.g. McKinnon) recommend a slower and more gradual process. The same divergence of views splits the orthodox and heterodox perspectives. The orthodox approach, as articulated by the World Bank (1994) and relying on recent research by Haggard and Webb (1993) on the political economy of adjustment, recommends: 1) speedy reforms to "foster the early emergence of new winners" and to enhance credibility that the government is committed to pushing the adjustment package through; 2) that reforms be bundled together rather than phasing them one at a time; and 3) that social safety nets should be initiated through complementary reforms to compensate the truly poor or those likely to become impoverished.

Sahn *et al.* (1994) make the interesting point that the analysts who favour a more gradual approach to adjustment do so on the grounds that "a slower implementation will soften the negative transitional impact on the poor and vulnerable". Since their research, in fact, shows that these policies do not inherently damage the poor, they argue that "the sooner these policies are undertaken, the better". The one caveat to this conclusion is that a recession damaging to all residents should be avoided at any cost. If that can be done, stabilisation and adjustment policies should be undertaken "as quickly and aggressively as possible".

Some heterodox writers not surprisingly favour a more gradual approach to adjustment — particularly with regard to the speed of import liberalisation. Cornia (1991) argues that sudden and sharp changes in protection rates tend to lead to de-industrialisation. Instead, he recommends "selective and temporary protection on a sliding scale (over a 5-10 year period)" as being more consistent with the goal of establishing an efficient manufacturing sector.

In conclusion, the case for the rapid implementation of a package interlinked with reforms is generally strong. However, where the institutional framework is inadequate (e.g. a backward banking system) and there is a shortage of skilled individuals (e.g. managers and entrepreneurs) a massive privatisation of state enterprises, for example, can only succeed if it is undertaken gradually. Although it is difficult to derive robust general lessons regarding the appropriate sequencing of reforms, it appears that export promotion should take precedence over import liberalisation. However, the two must be closely co-ordinated to avoid the anti-export bias of protectionist policies. The pace of import liberalisation must also be such that it does not "strangle" the agricultural and industrial sectors of crucial inputs. In addition, in order for structural reforms to be effective, they need to be accompanied (or preceded) by measures fostering greater internal market competition in both product and factor markets.

Issues Related to the Role of External Transfers and the Debt Overhang

There is no consensus on the appropriate role of external transfers in contributing to short-term stabilisation and long-term development objectives. In principle, this contribution could occur: *1)* indirectly, through conditionality leverage leading to the implementation of policy reforms conducive to the above objectives, and *2)* directly, by providing additional resources relaxing import and investment constraints. Mosley *et al.* (1991) found that while the effect of structural adjustment on national income is neutral, this neutrality is the result of two opposing forces. Policy reforms are positively correlated with national income while the latter is negatively correlated with increased external financing. The inference that is drawn is that the negative effect of external flows may be because countries use finance as a substitute for painful reforms[10]. The above evidence suggests that finance might delay or even discourage policy reform and thereby harm economic performance. A contrasting approach (favoured by many heterodox contributors) claims that external finance not only improves performance but is even more critical than the reforms themselves (Helleiner, 1992).

Focusing more specifically on issues related directly to balance-of-payments support, Sahn *et al.* (1994) identify three major reasons for balance-of-payments support: 1) the financing of current-account deficits during the transition period when imports increase faster than exports in a reforming economy (this is done so that sharp contractions of output are avoided and investment in the tradable sector can be more easily promoted); 2) the desire to leverage policy changes through conditionality of balance-of-payments loans; and 3) the support for debt service. CFNPP researchers are sceptical of the macroeconomic rationale for an indefinite continuation of balance-of-payments support. Such interventions, in their eyes, although necessary to restore equilibrium, should be phased out after some transitional period. Otherwise it may potentially, and ironically, conflict with the growth of exports. Currency devaluation and import liberalisation are normally designed to encourage exports.

> Yet, when foreign exchange is priced at its equilibrium value (another goal of most adjustment programmes), increased balance of payments support appreciates the real exchange-rate, diminishing the incentives for exporters ... If exports truly are the engine of rapid growth in the long run, increased balance of payments support could actually harm the poor and non-poor alike by reducing growth rates. (Sahn *et al.*, 1994, p. 159)

If the availability of foreign currency under a SAL acts as a substitute for generating export earnings — or at least reduces the incentives to rely on exports for the necessary foreign exchange — then the country loses the enormous potential externalities that are linked with export growth. First, exports constitute a conveyor belt for the import and adoption of new technologies. Secondly, by working with state-of-the-arts technologies, workers and engineers alike will benefit from the learning-by-doing and learning-by-looking processes that contributed so successfully to human capital and entrepreneurial skills — as the East Asian experience has clearly demonstrated. Furthermore the same authors argue that two other presumed reasons for balance-of-payments support, i.e. policy conditionality and debt-service support, are neither necessary nor optimal. Conditionality could be, and often is, linked to project lending, albeit with reduced leverage, and that relief could be provided to countries contingent on the pursuance of aggressive SSAPs.

The question of external funding cannot be analysed separately from the overall debt problem. The two are intrinsically linked. What matters for a given government is the amount of net transfers available (i.e. gross transfers minus debt amortisation). A recent study indicated that

> in [many low-income countries] the debt crisis has halted development ... Although financial difficulties are not the only barriers to development in these countries, no policy for growth in the short term could be contemplated without resolving the debt problem at the same time. (Berthélemy and Vourc'h, 1994, pp. 13-14)

The authors further argue that adjustment, although a necessary condition for getting out of the debt crisis, is not sufficient, however, "as the financial difficulties cannot be resolved without growth, and a revival of growth is not possible in the short term without relief from the financial constraints on the state budget and balance of payments". The authors outline a possible debt-relief strategy involving a co-ordinated approach between donors and debtors. The key components of such a strategy, on the donor side, would require consent by all creditors (to avoid the free-rider issue) and an equal (or equitable) sharing of the burden of debt relief. On the debtors' side, debt relief would be made conditional on the implementation of policies conducive to development.

In a 1994 OECD meeting on "Prospects for Debt Relief in Africa" attended by representatives of both donors and debtors, a few key strategic issues were discussed with only a limited consensus being reached. The following issues stand out in the resulting document: *1)* the African debt overhang should be dealt with on a case by case basis, *2)* the donor country governments should be willing to wipe out claims equivalent to $60 billion (the discounted real value of these claims is, of course, considerably less)[11], *3)* creditors should agree on the fairest possible distribution of the burden among themselves to avoid any free-riding, *4)* financial well-being of multilateral institutions must not be endangered, which implies that their principal shareholders, i.e. the rich countries, should be willing to meet the cost of cancelling these multilateral loans (OECD, 1994).

In conclusion, a massive debt-forgiveness exercise is required to reach a sustainable long-run financial situation for the highly indebted African countries. A strong case can be made according to which continuing access to external financing has already encouraged, and may continue to encourage and engender a dependency relationship — if not syndrome — inimical to a path of self-sustained development. However, debt relief should be made conditional on the continued implementation of adjustment policies *and* other complementary reforms crucial to the success of a long-term development strategy. The relief could be decided *ex post facto* based on an evaluation of the policy performance in such a way that successive tranches of debt relief would be released contingent on good policy.

Demographic Strategy

From a base of 210 million in 1960, the African population is projected to reach 700 million at the turn of the century and 1.3 billion in 2005. The average population growth rate is around 3 per cent a year; 20 per cent of the population are not yet 5 years old and 45 per cent are younger than 15 — implying dramatic increases in dependency burdens. Hugon (1993) has spelled out a number of implications and consequences of what he calls the demographic dynamics, that is: *1)* the proportion of children eligible to attend school out of the total population is 2.5 times higher than in industrialised countries with concomitant educational burdens, *2)* ecosystems continue to be harmed and depleted (e.g. through desertification, deforestation, and soil erosion), and *3)* the rural to urban migration continues to accelerate, often leading to urban pauperisation. Very few African countries have reached the demographic transition. Birth rates continue to be very high and stable.

Curiously, both the orthodox and heterodox approaches are almost silent on what would constitute an appropriate demographic strategy. Very few African countries have adopted population control (contraceptive) policies. Progress on this front appears literally critical if the larger output resulting from sound economic policies is not to be eroded away by population growth. An argument often heard is that contraceptive policies can only succeed if they are preceded by socioeconomic development (e.g. higher standards of living, improvements in maternal education). Evidence from very poor countries (such as Bangladesh) suggest that population-control measures can be implemented and lead to a significant reduction in the fertility and birth rates, slow growth notwithstanding. It appears that Africa cannot afford to wait for its demographic problem to be solved in a more or less automatic fashion in parallel with the development process. Aggressive contraceptive policies need to be designed and implemented right away.

Zimbabwe provides an interesting example of a country that has successfully embarked on a national programme of family planning. More than 800 civil servants cover the countryside with supplies of birth control pills and condoms and even a wooden replica of a key part of the masculine anatomy for demonstration purposes. The *New York Times* of 4 September 1994 reported that Zimbabwe even has a minuscule new export industry: it sells these wooden objects to family-planning programmes in other African countries for demonstrating the proper use of condoms.

Some Other Political Economy Issues

Borrower ownership stands out as a primary determinant of programme success (Johnson and Wasty, 1993). Many of the early programmes were seen by the recipients as being imposed upon the country by the World Bank. The greater the participation of the borrower in design and implementation of the programme, the greater the ownership, and hence the greater the likelihood of a successful outcome. This relationship between programme success and ownership can be subject to a *post hoc ergo propter hoc* type circularity argument: if the programme succeeds, then there was ownership, and if it falters, then ownership was absent. To circumvent such a difficulty, the Operation and Evaluation Department of the World Bank established a classification scheme where ownership is treated as a four-dimensional independent variable. For each dimension there are four levels reflecting the intensity of ownership, yielding a total of 16 possible ratings for each adjustment operation reviewed. The four dimensions of ownership are: *1)* locus of initiative, i.e. the extent to which the initiative is clearly the borrower's; *2)* the level of intellectual conviction among key policy makers; *3)* expression of political will by top leadership; and *4)* efforts towards consensus building among various constituencies. The statistical analysis of data (totalling 82 programmes in 38 countries — many in Africa) revealed a very strong positive relationship between programme outcome and borrower-ownership. Johnson and Wasty (1993) reached the following additional conclusions: *1)* virtually all instances of high borrower ownership were characterised by a "relatively" stable political environment irrespective of the nature of its political regime (Kenya and Malawi were countries that exhibited consistently high ownership), and *2)* perhaps the single most significant factor in government's ownership of the reform programme was the support of (or lack of opposition from) pressure groups toward their government's pursuit of reforms. For example, Ghana embarking upon its economic recovery programme, enjoyed the strong support of workers and students who hailed the revolutionary measures of the new government. Malawi, too, was successful in convincing domestic opposition — through a variety of instruments (like sharing of the profits of the state holding company) in favour of its populist platform.

Political economy of external aid. Structural adjustment can be looked at as a bargaining process between bilateral and multilateral donors, on the one hand, and debtor governments, on the other (Mosley and Toye, 1987). In particular, the survival of international financial organisations requires maintaining at least a certain minimum level of activity; once this condition is fulfilled, the "bureaucracy" of these organisations tries to go further. As Lafay and Lecaillon (1993) indicate, "If prestige, interest of the work, power and remuneration depend on the size of the administration concerned, the logical aim is to maximise the level of activity ... subject to a certain minimum probability that these loans will be repaid." Furthermore, they argue that the "bureaucratic" interest of international organisations and the "political" interest of the national governments are far from being contradictory: "Each of the participants in their negotiation has a direct interest in defining a conditionality that is both economically effective and politically feasible." One interpretation (not necessarily that favoured by the authors) is that both sides have a vested interest in following soft rules in their lending and borrowing behaviour, respectively. The credibility of the conditionality game needs to be enhanced — particularly if, as suggested above, debt relief is to be provided contingent on actual policy changes.

A final important political-economy issue is the degree of consensus for reform in the borrower countries. Generally reforms are seen by the dominant political constituencies (e.g. the political leaders, the civil service, parastatals and frequently urban workers) as involving substantial costs with few benefits. The urban élite, including civil servants, often stands to lose rents in the short run, hence civil servants have little incentive to implement most reforms. Lafay and Lecaillon (1993) have remarked that it is the behaviour of the "civil society" that determines the final degree of political feasibility of programmes. If a favourable coalition can be built, adjustment may succeed. The risks of failure are particularly grave in political regimes that combine the personalisation of power, the discretionary authority of the leaders, and clientelist redistribution. Another political-economy factor, in addition to borrower ownership and building broad-based consensus for reform, is the credibility of the government's commitment to reform. To support the programme, the civil service and the population in general must be convinced that the government's shift in economic policy is permanent and is not based on short-term incentives.

Conclusions

This chapter has been devoted to a comparison of the development experience of a number of Asian countries over the last four decades with that of sSA. Many policy elements and political economy factors that proved successful within the Asian context appear to be also applicable to Africa. In particular, the Southeast Asian model appears to be a relevant model for Africa to follow. The major findings are the following.

– The main reason why Asia grew faster than Africa between 1965 and 1990 is that it invested a much larger share of its GDP, i.e. 31 per cent as compared to 17 per cent for Africa. This poor investment performance resulted in a negative total factor productivity (TFP) growth in sSA compared to a large productivity growth of about 2.4 per cent per annum in Asia. TFP growth is largely determined by investment in education and other forms of human capital in addition to the adoption of modern technologies often linked to exports. On both counts, Africa lagged significantly behind Asia.

– The superior development record of Asia over the last three decades was analysed under three categories: *1)* patterns of governance and economic strategy, *2)* use of factor endowment, and *3)* components of development strategies. The major factors that were identified as accounting for the relative development success of Asia in contrast with Africa were: a) a somewhat greater degree of political stability; b) a much greater priority given to socioeconomic development (among other policy objectives) by the Asian regimes (in many cases rapid growth was essential to their survival); c) Asian leaders understood better than their African counterparts that in a rent-seeking environment "growing rents require growing economies"; d) the treatment of entrepreneurially able ethnic minorities was, on the whole, much more accommodating in Asia than in Africa; and e) the insulation of economic policy making from politics was much greater in Asia than in Africa, in particular through the establishment of relatively strong and independent institutions and reliance on a cadre of well-trained economic technocrats.

– With regard to factor endowment, Asia followed the dictates of dynamic comparative advantage much more closely than did Africa. Asia, at the outset, relied extensively on primary-products exports while continuing to concentrate on encouraging domestic food production. Asia, in contrast with Africa, continued to provide a gross flow of resources to agriculture to increase this sector's productivity and potential capacity of contributing an even larger return flow to the rest of the economy in the form of an agricultural surplus that could be used to finance the industrialisation process. In contrast, many African countries discriminated against both food crops and agricultural export crops through a variety of measures that were so extractive that they discouraged the growth of agricultural output.

- The existence of a better physical infrastructure and transportation network in Asia combined with less distortional price policies reduced transaction costs both for agricultural commodities sold in rural and urban markets and for manufactured inputs and consumer goods sold in the rural areas. The HPAEs in Asia did not suffer from the types of shortages of manufactured goods that were so prevalent in Africa in the 1980s.

- Asia's macro-economic management characterised by sound fiscal policies, conservative monetary policies and the maintenance of equilibrium exchange-rates contrasted dramatically with that of Africa.

The following recommendations appropriate to a sustainable long-term development strategy for sSA result from our analysis.

1. Agricultural and rural strategy

a) The case for unambiguous property rights is convincing. The issuance of land titles confers many advantages to owners. However, in certain settings, group titling might, in fact, be desirable and consistent with improving agricultural performance.

b) The case for complementary investment in agricultural research and physical infrastructure is compelling. Getting prices right is — at best — only one blade of a pair of scissors. In order to reduce the dilemma faced by adjusting countries about how to balance short-term cuts in public expenditures with the long-term need for improving the physical infrastructure and financing agricultural research, increasing the share of agricultural Sector Adjustment Loans (SECALs) while reducing that of generalised programme loans (SALs) in the World Bank lending portfolio suggests itself. Transfers imbedded in agricultural SECALs contribute directly to a tangible productive counterpart.

2. Industrialisation strategy

a) The case for removing discriminatory measures against the informal sector is compelling. For a long time to come, the informal sector in Africa must continue to play the role of a labour sponge and therefore should, at the very least, not be at a competitive disadvantage. Improvements in the urban transportation and distribution network would help reduce marketing and other transaction costs presently borne by small, informal enterprises.

b) An industrial strategy predicated on a "structured market" (i.e. reserving a share of credit and foreign exchange for small firms) and selective protection — as recommended by the heterodox school — raises all kinds of questions. In an environment characterised by limited technical know-how and administrative ability, rent-seeking and clientelism, and the lack of insulation of the civil service from politics;

such an industrial strategy appears doomed. Under those circumstances, as the NIEs in Asia demonstrated, it may be wiser to rely largely on more market- and free-trade-oriented policies and minimise interventionist policies.

c) Finally, the premise of the heterodox school that industries in sSA are not competitive needs to be put to the test. There is some — albeit limited — evidence so far that producers in some industries can compete in world markets.

3. Trade strategy

a) A number of heterodox authors expressed concern that the small size of most sSA countries is unsuitable for efficient import-substitution and propose the creation of regional trade agreements as a solution to this problem. The worldwide experience with relatively small regional trade agreements has been uniformly discouraging. If the whole of Africa could be integrated into one common market, it would, of course, increase the scope for trade creation; but such an arrangement might prove to be extremely difficult to implement in practice.

b) The scope for significant growth of primary products exports in sSA is limited. Africa has lost a significant share of most of these products to other regions and with appropriate policies, it should be able to recapture a part of these losses. Hence, the potential scope for African export growth of these commodities is higher than the very limited projected growth of world demand.

c) The solution in the long run, however, must lie in expanding manufactured exports. Important lessons can be learned from the gradual transition in export composition that occurred in Asia. An outward orientation centred on manufactured exports generates major positive externalities by contributing significantly to the human capital of workers and engineers operating new technologies and inter-industry and inter-sectoral spill-over effects.

4. Investment in human capital

The role of human capital as a critical component of a successful development strategy is unquestioned. In the light of the severe budgetary constraints faced by African governments, a case can be made for restructuring some aid flows towards education in the form of educational SECALs. Here again, as in the case of agricultural SECALs, external funds could be earmarked and directly channelled into projects and other activities in education and thereby contribute directly to human capital formation.

5. Speed and sequencing of policy reforms

The case for a rapid (as opposed to gradual) implementation of a package of interlinked reforms is strong. There are however settings in which a gradual implementation is called for. Although it is difficult to derive robust general lessons regarding the appropriate sequencing of reforms, it appears that export promotion should take precedence over import liberalisation. However, the two must be closely co-ordinated to avoid the anti-export bias of protectionist policies. The pace of import liberalisation must also be such that it does not "strangle" the agricultural and industrial sectors of crucial inputs. In addition, in order for structural reforms to be effective, they need to be accompanied (or preceded) by measures fostering greater internal-market competition in both product and factor markets.

6. Issues related to the role of external transfers and the debt overhang

A massive debt-forgiveness exercise is required to reach a sustainable long-run financial situation for the highly indebted African countries. A strong case can be made that continuing access to external financing has encouraged a dependency relationship in sSA that may be inconsistent with a viable long-term development strategy. The credibility of the conditionality game needs to be enhanced— particularly if debt relief is to be provided contingent on the implementation of actual policy reforms. Bilateral and multilateral donors should enter into a dialogue with different political constituencies and — within the narrow range of manoeuvrability available to them — try to shape their lending portfolios so as to foster coalitions favouring reforms.

7. The population explosion in sSA is in full swing

Very few African countries have reached the stage of demographic transition. Birth rates continue to be very high and stable. Curiously, both the orthodox and heterodox approaches are almost silent on what would constitute an appropriate demographic strategy. Africa cannot afford to wait for its demographic problem to be solved in a more or less automatic fashion in parallel with the development process. Aggressive contraceptive policies have to be designed and implemented immediately.

8. A number of additional political economy issues need to be considered

There is strong evidence that "borrower ownership" stands out as a primary determinant of the success of a stabilisation and adjustment programme. The greater the participation of the borrower country in the design and implementation of the programme, the greater the ownership, and hence, the greater the likelihood of a successful outcome. Four key dimensions of ownership have been identified as a) the extent to which the initiative is clearly the borrower's, b) the level of intellectual conviction among key policy makers, c) expression of political will by top leadership, and d) efforts towards consensus building among various constituencies.

From the standpoint of the political economy of external aid, structural adjustment can be looked at as a bargaining process between bilateral and multilateral donors, on the one hand, and debtor governments, on the other. Both sides may have a vested interest in following soft rules in their lending and borrowing behaviour, respectively.

Notes

1. This group consists of the "Four Tigers" — i.e. Hong Kong, the Republic of Korea, Singapore, and Chinese Taipei — and the newly industrialised economies (NIEs), i.e. Indonesia, Malaysia, and Thailand.

2. For country-specific information on the stock of education in both Asia and Africa, see Roemer (1994).

3. See Perkins and Roemer (1994).

4. The following quote from *The Economist*, which appears in Berthélemy and Morrisson (1989) is most revealing in this regard: "The point has been reached where money no longer has any use. If you give someone a dollar tip, it is returned with the request for two cigarettes instead."

5. See also Dorosh and Sahn (1993) for the significant contribution of off-farm income in total income of poor households in a number of sSA countries.

6. It should be noted that in January 1994, West African CFA countries signed a treaty establishing a monetary and economic union (*Union économique et monétaire de l'Afrique de l'Ouest*, or UEMOA) to integrate the functions of an economic union with those of the monetary union that was already in place (*Union monétaire de l'Afrique de l'Ouest*, or UMOA). Among other objectives, UEMOA is supposed to provide the framework for a better articulation of both economic and monetary policies within the region. The treaty took effect on 1 August 1994.

7. There is much counter evidence showing that small farmers growing export crops are not at a disadvantage (in terms of income or nutrition) compared to smallholders growing domestic food crops (see e.g. Kennedy, 1989).

8. The loss of these market shares was largely due to overvalued exchange rates and other policy-induced distortions.

9. Lall (1990) made a similar point in the context of industrial development in sSA. He argued that "the market may not always provide on time the skills which are eventually needed to achieve growth in individual industries."

10. As Demery (1993) notes, "There may .... be problems of multi-collinearity among the regressors in the specification adopted. The 'compliance with conditionality' variable is likely to be correlated with financial flows variables."

11. Demery (1993) indicates that the stock of debt in 27 SAP countries increased by $33 billion in 1985-91 to reach $64 billion dollars in 1991, and that it would require debt relief of about $15 billion to achieve a sustainable debt situation.

References

AHMED, R. and N. RUSTAGI (1984), "Agricultural Marketing and Price Incentives: A Comparative Study of African and Asian Countries", International Food Policy Research Institute, May.

AKIYAMA, T. and D.F. LARSON (1993), "Recent Trends and Prospects for Agricultural Commodity Exports in Sub-Saharan Africa", PPR Working Paper No. 348, World Bank, Washington, D.C.

BERTHÉLEMY, J.-C. and C. MORRISSON (1989), *Agricultural Development in Africa and the Supply of Manufactured Goods*, Development Centre Studies, OECD, Paris.

BERTHÉLEMY, J.-C. and A. VOURC'H (1994), *Debt Relief and Growth*, Development Centre Studies, OECD, Paris.

BEVAN, D., A. BIGSTEN, P. COLLIER, and J. W. GUNNING (1987), "Peasant Supply Response in Ration Economies", *World Development*, Vol. 15, No. 4, April.

BHADURI, A. (1993), "Alternative Development Strategies and the Rural Sector", *in* A. Singh and H. Tabatabai, eds., *Economic Crisis and Third World Agriculture*, Cambridge University Press for ILO, New York.

BIGGS, T., G.R. MOODY, J-H. van LEEUWEN and E.D. WHITE (1994), "Africa Can Compete! Export Opportunities and Challenges for Garments and Home Products in the US Market," Discussion Paper No. 242, Africa Technical Department Series, World Bank, Washington, D.C.

BLOCK, S.A. (1994), "A New View of Agricultural Productivity in Sub-Saharan Africa", *American Journal of Agricultural Economics*, Vol. 76, No. 3, August.

CORNIA, G.A. (1991), "Is Adjustment Conducive to Long-term Development? The Case of Africa in the 1980s," Centro Studi Luca d'Agliano, Development Studies Working Papers, October.

CORNIA, G.A., R. van der HOEVEN and T. MKANDAWIRE (1992), *Africa's Recovery in the 1990s: From Stagnation to Human Development*, St. Martin's Press, New York.

DE JANVRY, A., M. FAFCHAMPS and E. SADOULET (1991), "Peasant Household Behaviour with Missing Markets: Some Paradoxes Explained," *The Economic Journal*, Vol. 101, No. 409, November.

DEMERY, L. (1993), "Structural Adjustment: Its Origins, Rationale and Achievements", World Bank, Washington, D.C., June.

DOROSH, P.A. and D.E. SAHN (1993), "A General Equilibrium Analysis of the Effect of Macroeconomic Adjustment on Poverty in Africa", Cornell Food and Nutrition Policy Program Working Paper 39, Cornell University, Ithaca, N.Y.

HAGGARD, S. and S.B. WEBB (1993), "What Do We Know about the Political Economy of Economic Policy Reform?", *World Bank Research Observer*, Vol. 8, No. 2.

HAGGBLADE, S., T. HAZELL and J. BROWN (1989), "Farm-Nonfarm Linkages in Rural Sub-Saharan Africa", *World Development*, Vol. 17, No. 8.

HELLEINER, G.K. (1992), "The IMF, the World Bank and Africa's Adjustment and External Debt Problems: An Unofficial View", *World Development*, Vol. 20, No. 6.

HUGON, P. (1993), *L'Economie de l'Afrique*, Éditions la Découverte, Paris.

JAEGER, W.K. (1992), "The Effects of Economic Policies on African Agriculture", World Bank Discussion Papers.

JAMAL, V. and J. WEEKS (1993), *Africa Misunderstood or Whatever Happened to the Rural-Urban Gap?*, ILO, The Macmillan Press, London.

JOHNSON, J.H. and S.S. WASTY (1993), "Borrower Ownership of Adjustment Programs and the Political Economy of Reform," World Bank Discussion Paper, May.

KENNEDY, E. (1989), "The Effects of Sugar Cane Production on Food Security, Health, and Nutrition in Kenya: A Longitudinal Analysis", International Food Policy Research Institute, Washington, D.C.

LAFAY, J-D. and J. LECAILLON (1993), *The Political Dimension of Economic Adjustment*, Development Centre Studies, OECD, Paris.

LALL, S. (1990), "Education, Skills and Industrial Development in the Structural Transformation of Africa," Innocenti Occasional Papers No. 3, July.

LINDAUER, D.L. and M. ROEMER (1993), "Development in Asia and Africa: Legacies and Opportunities," HIID and CAER Discussion Paper No. 18, December.

MOSLEY, P. (1990), "Increased Aid Flows and Human Resource Development in Africa", Innocenti Occasional Papers No. 5, UNICEF, Florence.

MOSLEY, P. and J. TOYE (1987), "The Design of Structural Adjustment Programmes", Overseas Development Institute Conference on The Design and Impact of Adjustment Programmes on Agriculture and Agricultural Institutions. 10-11 September.

MOSLEY, P., J. HARRIGAN and J. TOYE (1991), *Aid and Power: The World Bank and Policy-Based Lending*, Volume 1, Routledge, London.

OECD (1994), "Prospects for Debt Relief in Africa", Abidjan, 9-10 June.

PERKINS, D.H. and M. ROEMER (1994), "Differing Endowments and Historical Legacies", *in* D.L. Lindauer and M. Roemer, eds., *Development in Asia and Africa: Legacies and Opportunities*, HIID, Cambridge.

PLATTEAU, J.P. (1990), *Land Reform and Structural Adjustment in SubSaharan Africa: Controversies and Guidelines*, Report prepared for FAO, Rome.

ROEMER, M. (1994), "Asia and Africa: Towards a Policy Frontier", Harvard Institute for International Development, CAER Discussion Paper No. 23, May.

SAHN, D.E., P. DOROSH and S. YOUNGER (1994), "Economic Reform in Africa: A Foundation for Poverty Alleviation", Preliminary draft, Cornell University Food and Nutrition Policy Program, Ithaca, N.Y., July.

STEWART, F. (1992), "Short-Term Policies for Long-Term Development", *in* G.A. Cornia, R. van der Hoeven and T. Mkandawire, eds., *Africa's Recovery in the 1990s: From Stagnation and Adjustment to Human Development*, St. Martin's Press, New York.

THOMAS, V., A. CHHIBBER, M. DAILAMI and J. de MELO, eds., (1991), *Restructuring Economies in Distress: Policy Reform and the World Bank*. Oxford University Press, New York.

THORBECKE, E., with C. MORRISSON (1989), "Institutions, Policies and Agricultural Performance: A Comparative Analysis", *World Development*, Vol. 17, No. 9.

VIVIAN, J.N. (1991), "Greening at the Grassroots: People's Participation in Sustainable Development", UNRISD Discussion Paper 22, Geneva, April.

WORLD BANK (1993), *The East Asian Miracle: Economic Growth and Public Policy*, Oxford University Press, New York.

WORLD BANK (1994), *Adjustment in Africa: Reforms, Results, and the Road Ahead*, Oxford University Press, New York.

Synthesis

*Jean-Claude Berthélemy and Jacques Lecaillon**

If it is true to say that the 1980s were "a lost decade in terms of development", this now familiar expression applies most accurately to sub-Saharan Africa, as is illustrated by just one of the many figures available: per capita GDP fell 15 per cent in this part of the world between 1977 and 1985.

It is now generally accepted that this failure resulted from a combination of past domestic policies and external shocks, which gave rise to a series of disequilibria and distortions that were incompatible with sustained growth. The external factors are well known: worsening terms of trade, a rise in real international interest rates, changes in net external transfers, worldwide recession and droughts. However, contrary to conventional wisdom, it now appears that external shocks were not the main causes of the poor socioeconomic performances in sub-Saharan Africa during that period: if this tentative conclusion is correct, poor policy regimes, at least until the mid-1980s, are more to blame for the situation than was previously thought.

This presents a real intellectual challenge, including for the OECD Development Centre. If the divide in terms of standards of living and demographic growth between western Europe and sub-Saharan Africa is tending to widen, with all the political, financial and migratory consequences that this implies, this is partly due to the fact that international organisations have not always been capable of providing effective recommendations, despite all the surveys and reports available, or that they have swamped African governments with contradictory evaluations and advice. While the cold war almost certainly played a role in these divergences, it must be recognised that the transposition to sub-Saharan Africa of theoretical models worked out for industrialised countries has meant that local institutions and behaviour patterns have not been given their rightful place when it came to implementing reforms or development policies.

* The authors would like to thank Robert Masumbuko for his invaluable help.

The African situation has shown that while it is useful to pursue ongoing analyses, there is a need to deepen them and, with the help of African experts and policy makers, to widen their scope to include the non-economic factors that influence the effectiveness and feasibility of the recommendations made to African countries.

Such reflections can be divided into the following stages:

–   sub-Saharan Africa's economic performance and prospects;

–   the diagnosis;

–   role of non-economic factors;

–   research proposals.

Sub-Saharan Africa's Economic Performance and Prospects

The economic performance for the 1980s is now familiar: although recourse to harsh adjustment plans was justified under the circumstances, the impact of these measures was mitigated and the medium-term growth prospects are still dismal.

1.   Erik Thorbecke has analysed the *macroeconomic performances in sub-Saharan Africa* in great depth. The following observations are based on the information contained in his report and illustrate some of the most striking aspects.

Average annual GDP growth rates fell overall in volume during the 1980s compared with the end of the 1970s. They continued to slide during the period in question. The evolution of per capita GDP became negative in the 1980s and in most instances performance was worse at the end of the decade than at the outset.

The *fall in savings and investment* as a share of GDP was one striking off-shoot of this trend. The drop worsened during this period with the ratio of gross investment to GDP declining from 21 per cent during the 1970s to around 16 per cent in the 1980s for most of the countries studied, while remaining steady at around 25 per cent on average for developing countries. The resulting slowdown in the industrial sector meant that the structural changes needed to diversify output and exports did not take place. The limited advances in the farming sector were not enough to cope with the demographic pressures during the same period.

The increase in poverty was one of the most important consequences of this lack of development: the number of poor (those whose income is not sufficient to cover their basic needs) is estimated to have grown by 64 per cent between 1970 and 1985. The resulting proportion of underweight children stands currently at around 30 per cent. As very few African countries have reached the stage of "demographic transition", the median population growth rate is somewhere in the region of 3 per cent. A lasting lower production growth rate inevitably leads to a fall in individual living standards. Demographic pressure can also lead to environmental damage (deforestation, desertification and soil erosion). In many cases, it speeds up migration towards urban areas, which in turn leads to urban pauperisation.

Whether or not the pressure exerted by population growth is one of the principal obstacles to development must therefore be considered. However, it is a very sensitive problem and opinions tend to be divided on the subject.

2. The macroeconomic environment was complicated even further by a series of disequilibria: unsustainable budget deficits, high inflation, overvalued exchange rates and foreign-exchange deficits, which meant that *stabilisation and structural-adjustment programmes* had to be implemented. While it is always difficult to evaluate the *impact of such programmes*, the countries concerned had succeeded in reducing government spending and slowing inflation by the end of the 1980s: in many cases, the exchange rates had become more realistic and budget deficits had been reduced.

However, *growth prospects for sub-Saharan economies* are still dismal: the World Bank forecasts average annual GDP growth rates for the region as a whole (1994 to 2000) at somewhere between 2.4 and 3.9 per cent which, although an improvement on past performance, is still less than the projected performances for developing countries as a whole (between 3.6 and 4.8 per cent).

The best case scenario would require a number of conditions that were looked at by Jeffrey Fine: economic recovery in developed countries, low interest rates, significant net transfers of capital to Africa; stability in commodity prices for African exports; improved world trade — all of which are difficult to bring together. What is more, the annual per capita growth rate for the best case scenario would not be higher than 1 per cent, due to population growth figures, which means that in ten years' time, living standards for a significant section of the population would be restored to those enjoyed in 1980 but with an increase in the number of people living in poverty.

Several speakers looked at the problem of *the link between economic policies and growth* from different angles. While stabilisation and adjustment measures are a necessary condition for new growth, they are not enough. Essentially, the purpose of these measures is to ensure an equilibrium. Inflationary disequilibria and the deficits that feed them must be eradicated for the same reason; growth in output is more dependent on supply than on demand; financial policy has a greater impact on prices than on output; as far as unemployment is concerned, it tends towards a natural level, which is determined by economic structures and the operation of the labour market.

The impact of such policies is vital for growth, especially on productive government spending and on macroeconomic variables such as real interest rates. Further reflection on the economic factors involved in sub-Saharan Africa is therefore essential.

The Diagnosis

New growth theories provide a basis for discussion of the causes of stagnation in sub-Saharan economies. Traditional theories stated than the long-term growth rate depended on population growth and productivity gains that made work more efficient: this rate was independent of savings. In other words, the long-term growth rate was "exogenous", in that it was neither influenced by the behaviour of the agents concerned (savings, investment, research) nor by economic policy (budget, taxation). This approach was unsatisfactory as it provided no explanation for the gaps between countries or the persistent differences in living standards. Recent studies have highlighted a strong correlation between the per capita capital growth rate and the change in techniques rate; countries with the fastest rates of development also have the highest rates of savings; countries that invest the most are better placed to use new data and skills. Studies on the sources of growth carried out since the end of the 1980s have stressed the role of capital in the widest sense of the term, including human capital and state infrastructure, the "external effects" of investment and the behaviour that encourages or discourages savings and the accumulation of capital.

1. *The strategic nature of investment* was stressed in several papers and statements. To illustrate this point, it was pointed out that the ratio of investment to GDP in Africa averaged 17 per cent between 1965 and 1990, whereas it was over 30 per cent in East and Southeast Asia during the same period. Based on these figures, it was calculated that growth in total factor productivity was positive in Asia (2.4 per cent per year) and negative in Africa (-0.4 per cent) over the same period. In this context, two themes were considered particularly significant because they implicate governmental responsibility:

– The first concerns the *development, or simply the maintenance of infrastructure*, which has been seriously neglected due to lack of funding. The lack of means of communication hinders market organisation and the operation of the pricing mechanism: transportation and distribution problems add to transaction costs that separate the production price from that paid by the end consumer. Whenever such costs increase, there is generally a corresponding decrease in trade; if they increase too much, trade in that product will cease altogether; in other words, a deterioration in the transport and distribution system will bring a country back to a subsistence economy. Distribution costs in Africa are extremely high compared to Asia.

– The second theme relates to *expenditure on education*, given the importance of human capital as a source of growth. Here again, there are major problems because of the high proportion of young people in a rapidly expanding population. Many countries have been obliged to give priority to training an élite to become public officials and modern-sector executives. However, these posts have now reached a saturation point and the most educated individuals are faced with unemployment or expatriation. The question that must now be faced squarely is whether the priority should not now be given to basic education and the eradication of illiteracy.

2.   One of the principal ideas in new growth theories is that investment (in the widest sense of the term) gives rise to *"positive externalities"*. It not only improves the productive capacity of a particular business or of individual workers, but also that of the businesses or workers with which they come into contact; this results in transfers of know-how or experience between those who use new techniques and explains why firms using advanced technologies are often located in specific zones or geographical poles.

This inevitably brings up the problem of creating industrial development poles, along with that of *spill-over effects and the factors contributing to the propagation of growth,* which were examined in the report by Jean-Paul Azam. Azam's paper brought up several types of questions:

–   A policy of export diversification and of effective import substitution without customs protection is obviously vital to the strengthening of the resilience of African economies to external shocks. From this standpoint, while an industrial-development policy may be desirable, it can not be based on the creation of an inefficient public sector as has been the case in the past. A strategy based on market forces and on the opening up of the domestic economy is certainly more conducive to growth, because it facilitates trade and makes economies of scale in output possible, stimulates productivity and facilitates technology transfers. However, it also imposes heavy constraints on economic policy with regard to exchange rates, for example.

–   The problem of *the location of growth poles and spill-over effects* then arises. To what extent can South Africa be a driving force and in which zone of influence? What other countries or regions have the same assets? Is it not true to say that existing borders, left over from the colonialist era, produce an artificial fragmentation of markets? Would the creation of vast free-exchange areas be enough to ensure the spread of growth-propagation and spill-over effects or should co-operation agreements and the creation of institutions to guarantee regional integration be encouraged instead?

–   The *channels* through which growth-propagation factors develop must also be identified. Is it a matter of investment in neighbouring countries with the corresponding problems of capital transfers? Do temporary or permanent labour migrations create a phenomenon of attraction towards these poles? Does increasing trade make economies of scale and a rise in living standards possible?

It was also recalled that pricing and marketing policies for agricultural products have prevented agriculture from generating a surplus that could be channelled into new activities. This example alone is enough to illustrate the role of political factors among the causes of blocked growth.

Role of Non-Economic Factors

Many African countries have had only a brief political history as a nation: independence left them with a normative model of the nation-state, which does not necessarily correspond to their customs or local cultural or ethnic diversity. The Western concept of the state is based on the existence of a coherent entity, capable of making decisions and ensuring that they are implemented; the basic image is that of an "all-knowing and benevolent despot", whose function is to improve the well-being of the group as a whole, with individuals and sub-groups abandoning all recourse to political pressure and violence. The state's main functions are to create the appropriate environment for the activities of the private sector, to produce and distribute essential public goods, to reduce major disparities in the distribution of income and to rectify market failures. The transposition of this model, which has already come under fire in the West, to lesser developed countries is clearly questionable, as it requires a degree of intervention that is completely beyond the capacity of the public sector, as Jeffrey Fine pointed out in his report. These countries did not have the stable socio-political environment required, the appropriate type of political institutions or the administrative skills needed.

1. *Instability in the socio-political environment* was cited as a risk factor likely to hold back national or foreign investment. While peace is not enough to guarantee growth, the threat of violence, which can in certain cases jeopardise the executive power, often plunges a country into a downward spiral of economic decline.

Initially, explanations of political instability in the widest sense of the term, ranging from collective protest movements (strikes, riots), to acts of civil war and irregular transfers of executive power (*coups d'état*), were based on the absence of cohesion in the civil society itself. Tribalism and the lack of a middle class to act as a buffer, the unequal distribution of land or access to education, the level of urban concentration or even the structure of the armed forces or the police are all possible elements that can ignite civil unrest. In years to come, given the pressure exerted by population growth, the problems of access to land and water and the large-scale migrations they cause will be an important potential source of conflict. However, the deterioration in the economic situation during the 1980s highlighted the role of economic variables in the strict sense of the term, particularly the growth rate of income and the inequality of its distribution. The influence of socio-political violence on the economy should not be overlooked either: riots, a civil war or a *coup d'état* and the disorganisation and uncertainty they create invariably lead to a slowdown in activity and frighten off investors. This may give rise to a "vicious circle" of political instability and economic recession.

2. *The type of institutions involved* also plays a role to the extent that, as Jean-Paul Azam pointed out, the means employed to deal with the situation — either repression or the redistribution of wealth to curry political favour — make it at least possible to ensure the survival of the executive power, if not maintain peace.

The type of political regime has long been at the core of reflections on the capacity of states to manage adjustment plans and to ensure economic development. Hypothetically speaking, an authoritarian state is considered to be more durable than governments that are subjected to the ballot box; those in charge generally remain in power for longer periods, which makes for greater continuity; decision making on technical grounds is easier because they are less dependent on public pressure; and authoritarian regimes are by definition better placed to crush protest movements. In practice, these hypotheses have not been borne out: no systematic link between the type of political regime and the capacity to implement a structural adjustment programme has been found. A regime's capacity to govern would appear to be less dependent on its constitutional form than on the actions and reactions between those in power and opposing social forces. These power struggles determine the feasibility of any development policy, the measures that can be taken and the speed of their application. On the other hand, and this is particularly true for sub-Saharan Africa, new problems arise when the power structure is replaced by what is known as "a transition to democracy" regime as a result of historical circumstances or outside pressures. The idea that the vote and the devolution of modes of governing should be in keeping with African traditions and culture was strongly emphasised, as the stakes involved could be the source of future conflicts.

"Weak" autocratic regimes are the most vulnerable, as they are based on a personality cult, the discretionary power of the country's leaders and selective redistribution. The political survival of governments depends to a great extent on their skill in maintaining the backing of elite groups through the distribution of economic "rents". In periods of crisis when the rents derived from mining, oil extraction or agriculture are reduced, such patronage is also reduced; in this way, an economic recession can lead to a political crisis.

The steps taken to stabilise the economy and particularly all those involving cutbacks, also mean that there is less money available to a government to secure its political future: in the same way, liberalisation policies and the down-sizing of the public sector mean fewer jobs, licenses or subsidies to distribute to supporters. This can lead to a selective withdrawal aimed at preserving rents to the detriment of those areas where public intervention is clearly vital (funding of infrastructure, education, the legal system).

Such a situation corresponds to a perverse extension of the behaviour known as *"rent-seeking"*. It is no longer a question of redistributing a surplus through patronage or modifications in property rights to such and such a group or category as a trade-off for their continued support. In fact, it is "predatory behaviour" since the maintenance of capital, a condition for future growth, is no longer guaranteed. Some theoreticians of rent-seeking have warned of the risks involved in a growing wastage of available resources, which disappear into a sort of "black hole"; the prospects are that economic decline will follow political paralysis.

3.   This prospect cannot be separated from the *efficiency of the administrative departments* responsible for drawing up and implementing the government's economic policy. Several speakers referred to the regrettable deterioration in the "administrative capacity" of African states as a result of the falloff in educational standards or the extension of rent-seeking behaviour.

While the quality and efficiency of any given administration depends on several factors, the need to ensure a genuine "integrity of national institutions" was stressed as being of the utmost importance by Jeffrey Fine, among others. The integrity and efficiency of institutions are essential for the *credibility of national policies* and several speakers saw this credibility as a basic condition for sustained growth. As a result, it is important to continue the work on the institutional changes that may be needed to reinforce such credibility; for example, how much autonomy should the central bank be allowed? To what extent are regional monetary agreements useful? In the context of the chronic political instability and the collapse of civil authority that exists in several countries, international organisations may be tempted to intervene more often and to tighten their control of the management process in these countries. However, by substituting themselves for the ineffectual authority in power, they run the risk of doing exactly the opposite of their original objective, making national leaders even less "accountable" and possibly creating "rejection reactions"? What is more, can we be sure that such interventions are exempt from bureaucratic prejudice? Several authors stressed the desire of Africans to control their own destinies and to look for solutions that correspond to their cultural background.

Research Proposals

In its previous research programmes, the Development Centre has endeavoured to draw lessons from the new theories of "endogenous growth", for both empirical studies and policy directions. The new theories have revived interest in analysis and especially in growth policy. While important work has already been done in this area, the topics discussed above clearly demonstrate that sub-Saharan African specificities are such that additional investigations are needed in order to address questions such as: What are the decisive economic factors to ensure a return to growth? How can the competitiveness of industries be guaranteed, especially in the sector producing labour-intensive goods? How can growth-propagation mechanisms be furthered in geographical terms, and hence in terms of regional co-operation? To what extent does the socio-political context, i.e. rent-seeking behaviour, violence, instability of institutions, hinder growth and what institutional reforms would be most appropriate to remedy the situation? These questions lead to a set of research proposals that form a coherent whole, which involve the participation of African experts and which would lead to specific policy recommendations.

1. Growth factors

The Development Centre has already analysed the economic performances of several countries on the basis of available time-series data.

The African case studies (Kenya and Senegal) have given rise to a *number of conclusions that need to be tested more systematically*. Among the most significant are:

a)   The content of education policy is at least as important for growth as the amount of expenditure on human capital, as measured by total expenditure on education.

b)   The financial system plays a role in the collection and mobilisation of savings towards investment, but this role would appear to be secondary at the outset of the development process.

c)   The objective of public investment is to remove obstacles to development, such as the lack of infrastructure: unfortunately, this factor is not easily detected in global time-series analyses. The same is true for the effects of trade policies due to the lack of data on the effective level of protection.

Additional data and analysis on these topics is needed before concrete recommendations can be made to African policy makers.

In terms of methodology, it would be useful to combine time-series studies and microeconomic analysis, so as to highlight *the microeconomic foundations of interpretations*. In this way, studies on enterprises or households would make it possible to measure the influence of infrastructure on activities and to reach a better understanding of household behaviour with regard to savings and investment, including investment in human capital. Research needs to be done on both African and, for comparative purposes, on Asian countries at comparable levels of development (India, Bangladesh).

2. International competitiveness and the labour market

Industrial development is an essential component of sustained growth, as it makes export diversification possible and because industrial activities can produce positive externalities that propagate growth. However, when dealing with the African context, this question must be treated with caution *because of the errors made* over the last 30 years. In fact:

a)   On the one hand, industrial policies have generally been based on the establishment of public enterprises, the efficiency of which has been more than questionable: they have been used by their respective governments to distribute rents (see point 4 below) and to pass on relatively high sums as remuneration to politically influential groups. Correcting these distortions would involve giving freer rein to market mechanisms and completing the privatisation of public companies.

b) On the other hand, the emphasis on industrialisation has been detrimental to the agricultural sector, creating serious distortions and disequilibria between the rural and urban areas. These disequilibria were partly wiped out by the adjustment policies of the 1980s.

However, obstacles still exist, notably *on the labour market.* In many countries, especially in French-speaking Africa, strict regulations still exist, ranging from setting a minimum wage to workforce management. When a country's principal comparative advantage is in production based on low-skilled labour, such a lack of flexibility is a serious obstacle to industrial development. From that standpoint, the 1994 devaluation of the CFA franc has made a substantial reduction in real salaries possible; it would be informative to evaluate the effects of this devaluation in a few years' time in order to see if it has had a positive effect on labour-cost constraints. Other measures, such as a minimum wage and how it is determined, or labour training policies such as those used in Chinese Taipei or Mauritius, should also be looked at in order to widen the range of options available to policy makers.

3. Regional co-operation

The progression of the growth process cannot be removed from its spatial context. It is obvious that the size of the economy conditions the possibilities of diversification as well as the scale of production: sub-Saharan Africa is a relatively fragmented part of the continent. In addition, disparities in growth and living standards could constitute a potential source of conflict and political instability (see point 5 below).

These drawbacks and risks can be attenuated through policies of regional co-operation. The existing economies have developed within borders that often do not reflect natural boundaries. The advantages of co-operation or free trade have not always been exploited to the full, generally for political reasons, and this has sometimes resulted in dramatic differences in per capita income among neighbouring countries. Such advantages also include heightened credibility for economic policies defined on a regional level, as well as a greater degree of autonomy with regard to pressures of all kinds.

Southern Africa is a good example of this (as is Israel for the Middle East). The political changes that have occurred there provide an opportunity to look into the advantages of regional co-operation and the obstacles that stand in its way. For example:

– Which investments (especially in infrastructure) and joint projects (relating to water or the environment) are expected to yield the greatest social benefits?

–   What are the main costs of the disparities between neighbouring economies (migratory flow, brain drain, peripheral desertification, potential sources of conflict)?

–   How can the losses and the risks involved in the transition periods be minimised and the security and a relative autonomy of individual states be maintained?

The answers to these questions could be enlightening for international organisations or donor countries, which are sometimes obliged to choose between efficiency and equity in the distribution of aid.

4. Rent-seeking

Rent-seeking behaviour is not peculiar to Africa, but it is probably more costly there in terms of development as the rents are being extracted from a more limited volume of resources.

In general terms, rent-seeking is tantamount to *a misappropriation of resources* that would otherwise have been used for development operations. It also introduces *costly distortions in the allocation of these resources*; for example, the advantages linked to state jobs encourages the most skilled members of the workforce to avoid production activities. It would appear that rent-seeking behaviour in Africa is more predatory than in other parts of the world, in that it involves an appropriation of the country's wealth without any attempt to ensure the growth or even the maintenance of the source of that wealth.

Studying such behaviour patterns is a difficult task, because of both the lack of information and the reluctance of political leaders to co-operate, as they are often deeply implicated themselves. *The development of a methodology* is therefore vital. A first step could be to try, through case studies, to measure the rents distributed in this way, either directly from government budgets, or indirectly through the effect of distortions arising, for example, from import restrictions or interventions in the foreign-exchange market. Little literature is available on these subjects at the present time: it needs to be updated and filled out in collaboration with the World Bank and local governments.

An assessment of the extent of rent-seeking activities based on an analysis of the distortion-inducing regulations would provide a better understanding of what type of political regime and economic context favours this behaviour. As far as political recommendations are concerned, emphasis should be placed on institutional reforms that could reduce rent-seeking behaviour or at least its economic cost, as well as on the types of measures and interventions that should be avoided or discouraged.

5. Conflicts and political instability

Redistribution linked to rent-seeking is sometimes used by those in power to ensure their political survival. They use this method to pacify their opponents and defuse potential sources of violence, instability and political risk. However, civil war and *coups d'état* are now regular means of taking over executive power; more than 80 per cent of the countries south of the Sahara have experienced at least one *coup d'état* since the mid-1950s. The number of such conflicts is a negative explanatory variable of the evolution of total factor productivity.

Future research should try to answer two types of questions:

–   On the one hand, what are the *main sources of civil violence?* Many non-economic variables are often cited: tribal or religious tensions, the type of political regime, the degree of repression, the rate of urbanisation, etc.; poverty or inequalities were barely considered in earlier studies. Case studies enabling a comparison to be made between relatively peaceful countries (Côte d'Ivoire, Kenya) with others, which have experienced periods of violence, would make it easier to isolate the decisive factors. The studies should try to pinpoint the nature and weight of economic variables in the origins of conflicts and define the policies that have made it possible to avoid such situations.

–   On the other hand, *which institutional reforms,* which types of measures and what forms of co-operation would lead to greater political stability and a balanced sharing of power?

Finding answers to such questions would be of interest not only to African policy makers, but also to the international community, as they could be used to establish the priorities for external aid.

List of Participants

Mr. Antonio Manuel DE ALMEIDA SERRA	Professor Instituto Superior de Economia e Gestão Universidade Técnica de Lisboa Portugal
M. Achi ATSAIN	Ministre de l'Emploi et de la Fonction publique Côte d'Ivoire
M. David ATSÉ	Administrateur principal Association des économistes de l'Afrique de l'Ouest Côte d'Ivoire
M. Jean-Paul AZAM	Professeur Centre d'études et de recherches sur le développement international, Université d'Auvergne France
M. Jean-Pierre BARBIER	Chef de Division Division Politiques, produits et procédures Caisse française de développement France
Mr. Gary BOMBARDIER	Deputy Assistant Administrator for Africa United States Agency for International Development United States

Mr. Enos S. BUKUKU	Personal Assistant to the Prime Minister and First Vice President of Tanzania United Republic of Tanzania
M. Gérald COLLANGE	Chargé de mission Division de l'Ajustement de la macro-économie Caisse française de développement France
Mr. Paul COLLIER	Director Centre for the Study of African Economies University of Oxford United Kingdom
Mr. Shanta DEVARAJAN	Chief Public Economy Division The World Bank United States
Mr. Jeffrey C. FINE	Independent Consultant Ottawa Canada
Mr. Stephen GELB	Department of Political Science York University Canada
Mr. Jan Willem GUNNING	Professor Faculty of Economics and Econometrics Free University of Amsterdam Netherlands
Ms. Joy E. HECHT	Consultant on Environment and Information Systems United States
M. Paul-Marc HENRY	Ambassadeur de France France
Mr. Mbaya KANKWENDA	Chief Economist, Regional Bureau for Africa and Chief, Regional Programme and Policy Analysis United Nations Development Programme United States

M. Solomane KONÉ

Centre ivoirien de recherche
économique et sociale
Côte d'Ivoire

Mr. Yasushi KUROKOCHI

Ambassador of Japan to Switzerland
Switzerland

Mr. Tim LANKESTER

Permanent Secretary
United Kingdom Department
for Education
United Kingdom

M. Ibrahim LOUTOU

Chargé de mission auprès
du Président-Directeur général
Air Afrique
Côte d'Ivoire

M. Alechi M'BET

Doyen
Faculté des Sciences économiques
et de gestion
Université nationale de Côte d'Ivoire
Côte d'Ivoire

Mr. Taye MENGISTAE

Centre for the Study of African
Economies
University of Oxford
United Kingdom

M. Christian MORRISSON

Professeur
Université de Paris I
France

Mr. Benno NDULU

Executive Director
African Economic Research
Consortium
Kenya

Mr. Louk DE LA RIVE BOX

Director
European Centre for Development
Policy Management
Netherlands

Mr. David E. SAHN

Food and Nutrition Policy Program
Cornell University
United States

Mr. Alexander H. SARRIS

Professor of Economics
Department of Economics
University of Athens
Greece

Mr. Lyn SQUIRE

Director
Policy Research Department
The World Bank
United States

Mr. E. TAPSOBA

Principal Economist (Africa)
United Nations Food and Agriculture
Organisation
Italy

Mr. Roberto TIBANA

Centre for the Study of African
Economies
University of Oxford
United Kingdom

Mr. Erik THORBECKE

Professor of Economics
Cornell University
United States

Mr. Arne TOSTENSEN

Senior Research Fellow
Chr. Michelsen Institute
Norway

National Delegations to the OECD

Germany	Mr. Horst WETZEL, Counsellor
Argentina*	Mr. Felipe A. CANDELLA, Counsellor, Embassy of Argentina to France
Austria	H.E. Mr. Peter JANKOWITSCH, Ambassador
	Mrs. Ulrike MAGLOTH, Minister-Counsellor
EC	DG VIII, Brussels
	Mr. L. GUERRATO, Director
	Mr. J. SEQUEIRA, Principal Administrator
United States	Mrs. Ann R. BERRY, Deputy Permanent Representative
	Mrs. Lee ROUSSEL, Minister-Counsellor
Finland	Ms. Kirsti AARNIO, Counsellor
France	M. Jean-Pierre DUBREUIL, Conseiller financier, Direction du Trésor, vice-Président du CAD
	Mme Bernadette LEFORT, Représentant permanent adjoint
	Mme Thérèse PUJOLLE, Chargée de mission, ministère de la Coopération
Ireland	Ms. Patricia CULLIN, First Secretary

Italy	Mr. Eugenio D'AURIA, First Counsellor
Japan	Ms. Mana KUMEKAWA
	Ms. Carol ANDERSON
Norway	Mr. Jan DYBFEST, Assistant Director General, Development Research, Ministry for Foreign Affairs
Netherlands	Mr. F. VAN DER KRAAIJ, Ministry for Foreign Affairs
Portugal	Mr. Mario A. LINO DA SILVA, Deputy Permanent Representative
	Mr. Luis BARROS, Second Secretary
	Mr. João RIBEIRO GOULÃO, Consellor
United Kingdom	Mr. Neil CHRIMES, Deputy Permanent Representative
Sweden	Mr. Mikael ERIKSSON, First Secretary
Switzerland	H.E. Mr. Eric ROETHLISBERGER, Ambassador, Chairman of the Advisory Board on the Development Centre

*   Argentina is a Member of the OECD Development Centre.

OECD Secretariat

Mr. Bernard WOOD — Director, Development Co-operation Directorate

Mr. Roy STACY — Head, Club du Sahel

Mr. Barrie STEVENS — Deputy Head, Advisory Unit on Multidisciplinary Issues, General Secretariat

Mr. Peter ELLEHOJ — Administrator, Statistical Systems Division, Development Co-operation Directorate

OECD Development Centre

Mr. Jean BONVIN — President

Mr. Ulrich HIEMENZ — Director for Co-ordination

Mr. Giulio FOSSI — Head, External Co-operation and Documentation

Mr. Jean-Claude BERTHÉLEMY — Head of Division

Mr. Jacques LECAILLON — Consultant

Mr. David ROLAND-HOLST — Principal Administrator

Mr. Hartmut SCHNEIDER — Principal Administrator

Mr. Dominique van der MENSRUGGHE   Administrator

Ms. Catherine DUPORT   Administrator

Mr. John BEGHIN   Visiting Fellow

MAIN SALES OUTLETS OF OECD PUBLICATIONS
PRINCIPAUX POINTS DE VENTE DES PUBLICATIONS DE L'OCDE

ARGENTINA – ARGENTINE
Carlos Hirsch S.R.L.
Galería Güemes, Florida 165, 4° Piso
1333 Buenos Aires   Tel. (1) 331.1787 y 331.2391
Telefax: (1) 331.1787

AUSTRALIA – AUSTRALIE
D.A. Information Services
648 Whitehorse Road, P.O.B 163
Mitcham, Victoria 3132   Tel. (03) 873.4411
Telefax: (03) 873.5679

AUSTRIA – AUTRICHE
Gerold & Co.
Graben 31
Wien I   Tel. (0222) 533.50.14
Telefax: (0222) 512.47.31.29

BELGIUM – BELGIQUE
Jean De Lannoy
Avenue du Roi 202 Koningslaan
B-1060 Bruxelles   Tel. (02) 538.51.69/538.08.41
Telefax: (02) 538.08.41

CANADA
Renouf Publishing Company Ltd.
1294 Algoma Road
Ottawa, ON K1B 3W8   Tel. (613) 741.4333
Telefax: (613) 741.5439
Stores:
61 Sparks Street
Ottawa, ON K1P 5R1   Tel. (613) 238.8985
211 Yonge Street
Toronto, ON M5B 1M4   Tel. (416) 363.3171
Telefax: (416)363.59.63
Les Éditions La Liberté Inc.
3020 Chemin Sainte-Foy
Sainte-Foy, PQ G1X 3V6   Tel. (418) 658.3763
Telefax: (418) 658.3763

Federal Publications Inc.
165 University Avenue, Suite 701
Toronto, ON M5H 3B8   Tel. (416) 860.1611
Telefax: (416) 860.1608
Les Publications Fédérales
1185 Université
Montréal, QC H3B 3A7   Tel. (514) 954.1633
Telefax: (514) 954.1635

CHINA – CHINE
China National Publications Import
Export Corporation (CNPIEC)
16 Gongti E. Road, Chaoyang District
P.O. Box 88 or 50
Beijing 100704 PR   Tel. (01) 506.6688
Telefax: (01) 506.3101

CHINESE TAIPEI – TAIPEI CHINOIS
Good Faith Worldwide Int'l. Co. Ltd.
9th Floor, No. 118, Sec. 2
Chung Hsiao E. Road
Taipei   Tel. (02) 391.7396/391.7397
Telefax: (02) 394.9176

CZECH REPUBLIC – RÉPUBLIQUE TCHÈQUE
Artia Pegas Press Ltd.
Narodni Trida 25
POB 825
111 21 Praha 1   Tel. 26.65.68
Telefax: 26.20.81

DENMARK – DANEMARK
Munksgaard Book and Subscription Service
35, Nørre Søgade, P.O. Box 2148
DK-1016 København K   Tel. (33) 12.85.70
Telefax: (33) 12.93.87

EGYPT – ÉGYPTE
Middle East Observer
41 Sherif Street
Cairo   Tel. 392.6919
Telefax: 360-6804

FINLAND – FINLANDE
Akateeminen Kirjakauppa
Keskuskatu 1, P.O. Box 128
00100 Helsinki
Subscription Services/Agence d'abonnements :
P.O. Box 23
00371 Helsinki   Tel. (358 0) 121 4416
Telefax: (358 0) 121.4450

FRANCE
OECD/OCDE
Mail Orders/Commandes par correspondance:
2, rue André-Pascal
75775 Paris Cedex 16   Tel. (33-1) 45.24.82.00
Telefax: (33-1) 49.10.42.76
Telex: 640048 OCDE
Internet: Compte.PUBSINQ @ oecd.org
Orders via Minitel, France only/
Commandes par Minitel, France exclusivement :
36 15 OCDE
OECD Bookshop/Librairie de l'OCDE :
33, rue Octave-Feuillet
75016 Paris   Tel. (33-1) 45.24.81.81
(33-1) 45.24.81.67
Documentation Française
29, quai Voltaire
75007 Paris   Tel. 40.15.70.00
Gibert Jeune (Droit-Économie)
6, place Saint-Michel
75006 Paris   Tel. 43.25.91.19
Librairie du Commerce International
10, avenue d'Iéna
75016 Paris   Tel. 40.73.34.60
Librairie Dunod
Université Paris-Dauphine
Place du Maréchal de Lattre de Tassigny
75016 Paris   Tel. (1) 44.05.40.13
Librairie Lavoisier
11, rue Lavoisier
75008 Paris   Tel. 42.65.39.95
Librairie L.G.D.J. - Montchrestien
20, rue Soufflot
75005 Paris   Tel. 46.33.89.85
Librairie des Sciences Politiques
30, rue Saint-Guillaume
75007 Paris   Tel. 45.48.36.02
P.U.F.
49, boulevard Saint-Michel
75005 Paris   Tel. 43.25.83.40
Librairie de l'Université
12a, rue Nazareth
13100 Aix-en-Provence   Tel. (16) 42.26.18.08
Documentation Française
165, rue Garibaldi
69003 Lyon   Tel. (16) 78.63.32.23
Librairie Decitre
29, place Bellecour
69002 Lyon   Tel. (16) 72.40.54.54
Librairie Sauramps
Le Triangle
34967 Montpellier Cedex 2 Tel. (16) 67.58.85.15
Tekefax: (16) 67.58.27.36

GERMANY – ALLEMAGNE
OECD Publications and Information Centre
August-Bebel-Allee 6
D-53175 Bonn   Tel. (0228) 959.120
Telefax: (0228) 959.12.17

GREECE – GRÈCE
Librairie Kauffmann
Mavrokordatou 9
106 78 Athens   Tel. (01) 32.55.321
Telefax: (01) 32.30.320

HONG-KONG
Swindon Book Co. Ltd.
Astoria Bldg. 3F
34 Ashley Road, Tsimshatsui
Kowloon: Hong Kong   Tel. 2376.2062
Telefax: 2376.0685

HUNGARY – HONGRIE
Euro Info Service
Margitsziget, Európa Ház
1138 Budapest   Tel. (1) 111.62.16
Telefax: (1) 111.60.61

ICELAND – ISLANDE
Mál Mog Menning
Laugavegi 18, Pósthólf 392
121 Reykjavik   Tel. (1) 552.4240
Telefax: (1) 562.3523

INDIA – INDE
Oxford Book and Stationery Co.
Scindia House
New Delhi 110001   Tel. (11) 331.5896/5308
Telefax: (11) 332.5993
17 Park Street
Calcutta 700016   Tel. 240832

INDONESIA – INDONÉSIE
Pdii-Lipi
P.O. Box 4298
Jakarta 12042   Tel. (21) 573.34.67
Telefax: (21) 573.34.67

IRELAND – IRLANDE
Government Supplies Agency
Publications Section
4/5 Harcourt Road
Dublin 2   Tel. 661.31.11
Telefax: 475.27.60

ISRAEL
Praedicta
5 Shatner Street
P.O. Box 34030
Jerusalem 91430   Tel. (2) 52.84.90/1/2
Telefax: (2) 52.84.93
R.O.Y. International
P.O. Box 13056
Tel Aviv 61130   Tel. (3) 546 1423
Telefax: (3) 546 1442
Palestinian Authority/Middle East:
INDEX Information Services
P.O.B. 19502
Jerusalem   Tel. (2) 27.12.19
Telefax: (2) 27.16.34

ITALY – ITALIE
Libreria Commissionaria Sansoni
Via Duca di Calabria 1/1
50125 Firenze   Tel. (055) 64.54.15
Telefax: (055) 64.12.57
Via Bartolini 29
20155 Milano   Tel. (02) 36.50.83
Editrice e Libreria Herder
Piazza Montecitorio 120
00186 Roma   Tel. 679.46.28
Telefax: 678.47.51
Libreria Hoepli
Via Hoepli 5
20121 Milano   Tel. (02) 86.54.46
Telefax: (02) 805.28.86
Libreria Scientifica
Dott. Lucio de Biasio 'Aeiou'
Via Coronelli, 6
20146 Milano   Tel. (02) 48.95.45.52
Telefax: (02) 48.95.45.48

JAPAN – JAPON
OECD Publications and Information Centre
Landic Akasaka Building
2-3-4 Akasaka, Minato-ku
Tokyo 107   Tel. (81.3) 3586.2016
Telefax: (81.3) 3584.7929

KOREA – CORÉE
Kyobo Book Centre Co. Ltd.
P.O. Box 1658, Kwang Hwa Moon
Seoul   Tel. 730.78.91
Telefax: 735.00.30

MALAYSIA – MALAISIE
University of Malaya Bookshop
University of Malaya
P.O. Box 1127, Jalan Pantai Baru
59700 Kuala Lumpur
Malaysia   Tel. 756.5000/756.5425
                            Telefax: 756.3246

MEXICO – MEXIQUE
Revistas y Periodicos Internacionales S.A. de C.V.
Florencia 57 - 1004
Mexico, D.F. 06600   Tel. 207.81.00
                            Telefax: 208.39.79

NETHERLANDS – PAYS-BAS
SDU Uitgeverij Plantijnstraat
Externe Fondsen
Postbus 20014
2500 EA's-Gravenhage   Tel. (070) 37.89.880
Voor bestellingen: Telefax: (070) 34.75.778

**NEW ZEALAND
NOUVELLE-ZÉLANDE**
GPLegislation Services
P.O. Box 12418
Thorndon, Wellington   Tel. (04) 496.5655
                            Telefax: (04) 496.5698

NORWAY – NORVÈGE
Narvesen Info Center – NIC
Bertrand Narvesens vei 2
P.O. Box 6125 Etterstad
0602 Oslo 6   Tel. (022) 57.33.00
                            Telefax: (022) 68.19.01

PAKISTAN
Mirza Book Agency
65 Shahrah Quaid-E-Azam
Lahore 54000   Tel. (42) 353.601
                            Telefax: (42) 231.730

PHILIPPINE – PHILIPPINES
International Book Center
5th Floor, Filipinas Life Bldg.
Ayala Avenue
Metro Manila   Tel. 81.96.76
                            Telex 23312 RHP PH

PORTUGAL
Livraria Portugal
Rua do Carmo 70-74
Apart. 2681
1200 Lisboa   Tel. (01) 347.49.82/5
                            Telefax: (01) 347.02.64

SINGAPORE – SINGAPOUR
Gower Asia Pacific Pte Ltd.
Golden Wheel Building
41, Kallang Pudding Road, No. 04-03
Singapore 1334   Tel. 741.5166
                            Telefax: 742.9356

SPAIN – ESPAGNE
Mundi-Prensa Libros S.A.
Castelló 37, Apartado 1223
Madrid 28001   Tel. (91) 431.33.99
                            Telefax: (91) 575.39.98

Libreria Internacional AEDOS
Consejo de Ciento 391
08009 – Barcelona   Tel. (93) 488.30.09
                            Telefax: (93) 487.76.59

Llibreria de la Generalitat
Palau Moja
Rambla dels Estudis, 118
08002 – Barcelona
             (Subscripcions) Tel. (93) 318.80.12
             (Publicacions) Tel. (93) 302.67.23
                            Telefax: (93) 412.18.54

SRI LANKA
Centre for Policy Research
c/o Colombo Agencies Ltd.
No. 300-304, Galle Road
Colombo 3   Tel. (1) 574240, 573551-2
                            Telefax: (1) 575394, 510711

SWEDEN – SUÈDE
Fritzes Customer Service
S–106 47 Stockholm   Tel. (08) 690.90.90
                            Telefax: (08) 20.50.21

Subscription Agency/Agence d'abonnements :
Wennergren-Williams Info AB
P.O. Box 1305
171 25 Solna   Tel. (08) 705.97.50
                            Telefax: (08) 27.00.71

SWITZERLAND – SUISSE
Maditec S.A. (Books and Periodicals - Livres
et périodiques)
Chemin des Palettes 4
Case postale 266
1020 Renens VD 1   Tel. (021) 635.08.65
                            Telefax: (021) 635.07.80

Librairie Payot S.A.
4, place Pépinet
CP 3212
1002 Lausanne   Tel. (021) 341.33.47
                            Telefax: (021) 341.33.45

Librairie Unilivres
6, rue de Candolle
1205 Genève   Tel. (022) 320.26.23
                            Telefax: (022) 329.73.18

Subscription Agency/Agence d'abonnements :
Dynapresse Marketing S.A.
38 avenue Vibert
1227 Carouge   Tel. (022) 308.07.89
                            Telefax: (022) 308.07.99

See also – Voir aussi :
OECD Publications and Information Centre
August-Bebel-Allee 6
D-53175 Bonn (Germany)   Tel. (0228) 959.120
                            Telefax: (0228) 959.12.17

THAILAND – THAÏLANDE
Suksit Siam Co. Ltd.
113, 115 Fuang Nakhon Rd.
Opp. Wat Rajbopith
Bangkok 10200   Tel. (662) 225.9531/2
                            Telefax: (662) 222.5188

TURKEY – TURQUIE
Kültür Yayinlari Is-Türk Ltd. Sti.
Atatürk Bulvari No. 191/Kat 13
Kavaklidere/Ankara   Tel. 428.11.40 Ext. 2458
Dolmabahce Cad. No. 29
Besiktas/Istanbul   Tel. (312) 260 7188
                            Telex: (312) 418 29 46

UNITED KINGDOM – ROYAUME-UNI
HMSO
Gen. enquiries   Tel. (171) 873 8496
Postal orders only:
P.O. Box 276, London SW8 5DT
Personal Callers HMSO Bookshop
49 High Holborn, London WC1V 6HB
                            Telefax: (171) 873 8416
Branches at: Belfast, Birmingham, Bristol,
Edinburgh, Manchester

UNITED STATES – ÉTATS-UNIS
OECD Publications and Information Center
2001 L Street N.W., Suite 650
Washington, D.C. 20036-4910 Tel. (202) 785.6323
                            Telefax: (202) 785.0350

VENEZUELA
Libreria del Este
Avda F. Miranda 52, Aptdo. 60337
Edificio Galipán
Caracas 106   Tel. 951.1705/951.2307/951.1297
                            Telegram: Libreste Caracas

Subscription to OECD periodicals may also be
placed through main subscription agencies.

Les abonnements aux publications périodiques de
l'OCDE peuvent être souscrits auprès des
principales agences d'abonnement.

Orders and inquiries from countries where Distribu-
tors have not yet been appointed should be sent to:
OECD Publications Service, 2 rue André-Pascal,
75775 Paris Cedex 16, France.

Les commandes provenant de pays où l'OCDE n'a
pas encore désigné de distributeur peuvent être
adressées à : OCDE, Service des Publications,
2, rue André-Pascal, 75775 Paris Cedex 16, France.

7-1995

OECD PUBLICATIONS, 2 rue André-Pascal, 75775 PARIS CEDEX 16
PRINTED IN FRANCE
(41 95 13 1) ISBN 92-64-14647-4 - No. 48329 1995